MW01036197

We've Moved!
Stephen's Hope Foundation, Inc.
P.O. Box 5943
Naperville, IL 60567-5943
Phone #: (630) 235-2245
www.StephensHope.org

A portion of the proceeds from the sale of this book goes to Pangaea, Inc., a not-for-profit organization, to support the care of children with disabilities and their families. For further information, visit the *Eagle Doctor* website at eagledoctor.com or write to Pangaea, Inc., 226 Wheeler Street South, Saint Paul, MN 55105-1927 USA.

Stories of Stephen,
my child with special needs

Eagle Doctor

Chrissy L. Nelson
Windwalker

Prologue by

Hunter (Patch) Adams, MD

PANGAEA

Saint Paul

Cover: Eagle drawing by Blake Deaton at age 8

International Standard Book Numbers
Hardcover 1-929165-02-1
Paperback 1-929165-05-6

Library of Congress Cataloguing-in-Publication Data

Nelson, Chrissy L., 1954-
  Eagle doctor : stories of Stephen, my child with special
needs / Chrissy L. Nelson (Windwalker).
    p. cm.
  ISBN 1-929165-02-1 (hardcover : alk. paper) —
  ISBN 1-929165-05-6 (pbk : alk. paper)
  1. Physically handicapped children—United States.
  2. Parents of handicapped children—United States.
  3. Special needs adoption—United States. I. Title.

HV904.N45 1999
362.4'083'0973—dc21   99-048932

WorldWideWeb

pangaea.org

Published in the United States of America
Printed in Canada
P A N G A E A
1999

On my ninth birthday
my mother gave me a book of poems.
Inside the cover she wrote,
"Happy Birthday, Chris. May you write a book such as this
someday."

My mother is my best friend.
She is my comrade and counselor.
She is my hero.

Before my father died last year he said,
"It's time to write your book. Do it for your mother,
it will make her smile."

Mom, I dedicate this book to you
in memory of dad.
I love you.

Contents

Introduction

On August the fifth, 1986, I was in Poplarville, Mississippi, canoeing with friends. While we portaged back up the river to our vehicle, I lost my balance and grabbed a tree branch to steady myself. Upon that branch, a water moccasin lay sunning itself. I was snakebit. Hours later I sat in the Emergency Room at the local hospital and listened as the doctor said, "God must want you for something. The amount of venom you had in your system should have killed you."

On August the fifth, 1986, in Minneapolis, Minnesota, Stephen Michael Rondell was born. Two years later we met and continued our lives together.

For eleven years I have witnessed God's grace in action. A beautiful boy, sinless, has grown into a young man, despite countless acute, life-threatening crises. His will to live exceeds any imaginable desire that I have experienced. He thrives on love. He mirrors God.

It is my privilege to bring you his life in this legacy of words. My prayer is that through these words, his life will reflect honor, bravery, serenity, joyfulness, and kindness to all who cross his path.

Prologue

When I was first asked to read this book and write a prologue—I winced, knowing I had no time to do it. But I had read some articles about Chrissy and Stephen and love this kind of love, so I said send it to me. I could hear in Chrissy's voice a quality of tenderness I thrive on. It arrived the next day and I decided to read a few pages and hours later, still reading, felt ready and desirous to write a prologue.

How I wish all politicians had the courage and love to care for an individual as Chrissy has for Stephen—for let's say five years—before they can run for election. How they need to understand that people who must have assisted caring are not burdens or responsibilities but vital human beings, often with a kind of humility and appreciation I've not seen in any politicians in my lifetime. This is not a story of Chrissy sacrificing her life for poor Stephen. This is a love story—a regular old, beautiful, mutual love between two people. I'm sure Chrissy lives the truth that she feels like she is the lucky one here. There is a quality of innocent, full disclosure in Chrissy's language that inhibits any from thinking she is sentimental, exploitative or exaggerating. She is simply reporting stories of their incredible love, maybe in hopes that readers can find this kind of love in their own lives.

Here is a strong political treatise challenging everyone who reads it to look inside and wonder if they have this kind of love in their life, either in the giving or receiving (or both in this case). Here is a confrontational challenge to selfishness in favor of joyful service and an equally loud voice shouting that Chrissy is getting as much or more from the relationship. One can tell quickly that however much concern and pity we may have for Chrissy's situation (and Stephen's), it isn't long before everyone is inspired by them— even maybe wishing love was so deep in their own lives. Chrissy and Stephen throw the word "can't" away.

Inherent in this small, beautiful community of two are ideas that when lived could bring peace and justice to our society. Those ideas could close all nursing homes and custodial dwellings and insist on creating communities where the intention is that all feel cared for in this way—for the deep pleasure of all concerned.

Currently we have a society with widespread loneliness, fear, anxiety, and depression. It makes sense, in this context, that when their elders or disabled are needing care, they are placed in institutions. And it makes sense that Chrissy and Stephen's story, in this context, looks like a garden—lush and sweet—without the gray. What Chrissy and Stephen represent is potential in human relations.

Hear their tale and imagine yourself loved in this way. Imagine yourself loving this way and it being intensely shared. I'd suggest these may be the truths found at the bottom of all thoughts. Humans need love and fun in their day-to-day lives. This is a composition of love and fun in two people that is clearly a masterpiece.

So here is a handbook. If you want a society free of violence and injustice, come here to *Eagle Doctor*. If you want a course in building community, here's how to lay a brick and a brick and a brick. Maybe we could live in a world where this kind of caring is commonplace and simply a natural part of our culture. So often we will ask "Where do you get your energy?" This book's answers are presented to readers so clearly and openly that all that is left to do is the doing. Here is the proof that anything can happen—so goodbye "impossible."

There is a feast of encouragement here for one's own dreams if one wants to write this kind of composition. I could tell with every story that I wanted to read the next one.

Is this an appropriate clinical report for testing the inherent value of love? Historically the healing power of love has had such remarkable qualities that often something so extraordinary happens that to evaluate it, the scientist has to call it a miracle. Maybe, rather than a miracle, it is simply the results of regular old love or a particular situation. That's what I felt from this book, which is less a tale of great courage than an invitation to the beautiful world of love.

I am so thankful that this hope sandwich is to be served up soon. I will recommend it to all who suffer and are caring for those who suffer. I will recommend it to all who quest for peace and justice on Earth. I have looked in this book and can see that it can happen.

Hunter (Patch) Adams, MD
Gesundheit! Institute
Arlington, VA

Acknowledgments

With heartfelt thanks to

Stephen—for constant encouragement to write his story;

My family—for endless love and support, even in the shadow of death;

Uncle Billy and Stephen's nurses—for working extra hours while I transformed Stephen's life into words;

My many friends and neighbors—for much laughter and friendship;

Fellow writers and editors—for counsel and a shoulder to cry on.

And most of all, to my friend and mentor *Bonnie,* for providing me with the tools to write Stephen's story, diligent guidance, boundless energy, and the kindest friendship this side of heaven.

CLN
Naperville, IL

Love children especially,
for like angels
they too are sinless,
and they live to soften
and purify our hearts
and, as it were,
to guide us.

Dostoevsky

God's Quilting

Bouncing on my grandfather's bed was a special treat. This time I bounced softly, because he was very ill.

My father had answered the telephone that evening in October. My family was gathered at the big kitchen table enjoying my mother's delicious farm cooking. A look of concern had come over dad's usually cheery countenance. Soon my brothers and sisters and I were dressed and loaded into the '57 Buick. We rode with mom and dad to grandma's house.

We arrived and everyone looked miserable. We learned that my grandfather was "making his last trail ride to heaven."

"Mom," I asked, "why is everyone so sad? In heaven grandpa can ride his horse all day long. He likes that."

My mother bent down to me, mussed my brown curls and tenderly said, "Grandpa will be the happiest he has ever been. We're just going to miss him, that's all."

One by one my dad, my mom, and my brothers and sisters all took turns sitting on grandpa's bed and talking to him. I was last. I had been hiding under grandpa's bed. No one saw me sneak into his bedroom, so I tucked myself under his high bed and listened quietly. If grandpa was going away, I wanted to spend every single minute possible with him.

"Chrissy, where are you?" Mom and dad were getting a bit frustrated; I could tell by their voices. When they all walked upstairs to try and find me, I crawled out from under grandpa's bed. "Little Chrissy, I knew you were in here all the time."

I climbed up onto the bed into his warm embrace.

"Grandpa, I don't want you to go away," I said.

He brushed the hair from my eyes while holding me in his arms and kissed my cheek. He pulled me close to his side and covered me with the white patchwork quilt that grandma had made for him. We lay in his bed, just the two of us. I held my grandpa tightly, thinking that if I held him real close he couldn't go anywhere. At least, not without me.

Soon my mom and dad were standing around grandpa's bed. My grandma sat by his side. Grandpa looked at me and said, "I'll miss you, too, little Chrissy, but I will always watch over you. Now tell me, what will I be watching you do? What do you want to be when you get bigger and stronger?"

A roar of laughter rose in the room when I said, "I want to be the mother of six boys." Grandpa hugged me and said, "Don't ever let go of your dream."

A few days later my grandfather died. I wrapped my dream into his white quilt and set it in the middle of my bed.

~~~

I reminisced about this scene as the ambulance I was riding in sped along. The countryside was brilliant at that time of year. The fall leaves blazed reds and oranges and the air shouted through the treetops. The ambulance swayed back and forth like an empty hammock caught in a windstorm. We would drive to the hospital today, grounded from flying our chopper due to the high winds. My paramedic partner was driving. I used the time to prepare both mentally and physically for the patient we would be transporting.

This had been my day off; at least it was supposed to have been. An unusual flurry of transports was taking longer then anticipated due to the prevailing high winds. Reluctantly I had agreed to help on this one. Caring for patients in an ambulance—air or ground—is not a glamorous profession, as some might think. Limited moving space creates a difficult arena in which to care for needy people. We often referred to the ambulance as the "swinging metal box."

We knew very little about the patient we were going to bring to the University of Minnesota, where she was to receive more advanced care than she could obtain in her small, hometown hospital. As the ambulance made its way on the rural roads, I swallowed hard and tried to keep my emerging tears at bay.

A few hours earlier, at a routine follow-up appointment with my doctor, I had heard the dreaded word: cancer.

"It appears to be contained and I think we got it all, but it will be very unlikely that you will ever have children of your own. Let's talk about your options."

Hearing that had stunned me. I shook the doctor's hand, said thank you and fled his office. I ran home and sat on the floor, wrapped up in my grandfather's quilt. That's where I was when the phone rang with the plea for help at work.

"Don't ever let go of your dream," my grandfather had said. The words tore at my soul, shredding my reason for living. Somehow I would find peace in this, someday this would make sense. Someday understanding would quell the waves of grief—but definitely not today.

We arrived at our intended destination after a bumpy and swinging four-and-a-half-hour ride. We backed into the ambulance garage and, removing the stretcher and needed supplies, entered the hospital. Usually the patients are in pretty bad shape by the time we arrive—that's why we transport them. Our arrival was met with relieved looks, handshakes and hugs.

The intensive care doctor orchestrated a huddle in a small office adjacent to the Intensive Care Unit (ICU). There we learned that our patient was a young girl who had been picked up early that morning at a clinic where she had had an attempted abortion. Something went wrong and now she, herself, clung to life.

Feeling nauseated, I sat down on a stool. One of the attending doctors gave me a glass of cold water and continued his briefing. He ended the report, explaining to us that he would not be able to ride with us back to Minneapolis, as previously planned. Another accident demanded his attention.

I could hardly believe what I had heard. Not only did we have a very sick patient to care for, she was a young girl who had attempted to abort her own child on the same day that I found out my lifelong dream to have children had ended. I shook my head and considered shaking my fist at God.

Entering the young girl's room, we were greeted with open arms. "I'm so glad you are here. She is so young. We don't know if she'll pull through or not."

Intensive training as nurse and paramedic flew into high gear as we worked to stabilize this young girl. My own emotions and personal reality would have to wait.

Before we left the hospital, I stopped by the Family Waiting Room to talk with her parents. The familiar look of desperation coupled with fear commandeered their faces. "Will she be okay?" they wondered. I gave them a lengthy report about her medical condition and the treatment we would be giving her en route to the hospital. We would be in constant radio contact with her family physician and the University of Minnesota Hospital. She would receive the best care we could offer.

Her father walked with me to the ambulance doors. We loaded his precious daughter into the ambulance and as the doors closed he handed me a white quilt with purple flowers on it. He said, "My grandmother made this quilt for my daughter to give to her first child. We'll never know him now, but take this. Accept it from my family. If my daughter survives I have you to thank. Dreams of my grandchildren are wrapped up in this quilt. Here, take it."

Struggling with the professional principle that gifts are not expected nor accepted, I stood frozen. Here was this man offering me a gift from his heart and, because of medical ethics, I couldn't accept it. He stood before me in tears with his hand on the window of the ambulance door. My partner, also one of the "bosses," walked to the back of the ambulance, took my hands and put them under the quilt. He smiled at the man and said, "Thank you."

I already had one precious quilt from my grandfather; this day God added another.

Exceptionless Child

by Kathleen Hogan

If you touch me soft and gentle
If you listen when I'm blue
If you read my eyes and smiles
Then I'll work for you.

If you know just what you're doing
If you like me I will know
Realize I am a person
Then I can really grow.

I learn in different ways sometimes
To talk and move and read
I like to play the same way, though,
And get the things I need

If it scares you when you see me
Makes you sad or turn away
Stop looking at me through your eyes
And sense what's me inside

Feel okay and be my friend
Don't worry what to do
Inside me there's a light that shines
Just like the one in you

From *OURS* magazine, June 1984.
Kathleen Hogan is a physical
therapist working for Oregon's
Crippled Children's Division.

He's Back

It's Christmas. Come on, Chris, you have to have one," Alli insisted as she handed me a candy cane. Her hospital room was decorated to celebrate Christmas. Surgical ties held colorful ornaments; candy canes were hooked onto every available protrusion; and oxygen tubing was filled with penlights on each end, resembling Obewankanobe laser swords. Life Saver candies were strung across cardiac monitors in every corner. Christmas carols were heard throughout the room. Wheels on chairs were decorated with red and green crepe paper; and red bows adorned Alli's and roommate Latasha's hair.

Snow shapes visible on the inside windows sheltered this room from the main unit area. Icicles dripped over the windows outside. Alli and Latasha were heading out of the room to join the Christmas carolers. Frosted sugar cookies in bell and star shapes awaited them. It was nearly Christmas Eve.

I stayed in the room to wrap the final presents. Placing them under the tree in the middle of the room, I paused to look at Stevie's empty crib. Forty-eight hours earlier he had been transported to the intensive care unit at Minneapolis Children's Hospital for stabilization of pneumonia. I returned to his hospital room to find his bed exactly as it had been left when they took him away. The same sheets, the same bandages, the same tubing lay in his crib, his toys and decorations motionless at his bedside. Everything was just as it had been when I went off duty two days earlier.

The room phone rang. "Hi, Chris. It's Dr. G. I just thought

you might want an update on Stevie. He didn't handle being placed on the ventilator, but his oxygen saturation is better and his pneumonia is responding to the antibiotics. We're going to keep him a few days until he turns around. Merry Christmas."

I felt happy with the news of his recovery, but sad that no one had come to get his toys and Christmas decorations. Christmastime has always been full of family and the exchange of beauty for me. I changed the sheets in his crib and finished wrapping his present. I felt a little better knowing that they would greet him when he returned.

I turned away from Stevie's crib and walked toward the door to join Alli and Latasha, who were enjoying the Christmas festivities. The happy Christmas celebrations of my childhood, all filled with joy and people, played through in my mind. Abruptly I stopped. Children should not be alone on Christmas. Stevie needed a friend. That night, Christmas Eve, I would take his belongings to him.

Latasha returned to the room to get a present she had made for Pat, our head nurse. Seeing me pack up Stevie's things she asked with grave concern, "Is Stevie an angel?" Hugging her, I said no, he just needs his things. She maneuvered her wheelchair around the Christmas tree and headed toward the nurse's station with her brightly wrapped present. I smiled as I saw her give it to Pat. Latasha had made a picture with a paintbrush in her teeth after we had read the story of Joni Erickson Tada. We were proud of her accomplishment.

All of Stevie's belongings fit into one small box. I closed it and joined Alli and Latasha. Having finished singing seven made-up verses of "Jingle Bells," we headed back to their room. It was time for Alli and Latasha to get back into bed.

The Christmas celebration would continue. We had plans to read the Christmas story before sleep time. Pat came in and said, "Chris, I need to give you an admission. I am really sorry but I didn't know about it either and this is the only room with a spare bed. I will help you when I'm done with rounds. The admit should be here in a half hour. Alli and Latasha can stay up a bit longer. I'll help you get them into bed after the admit gets settled." Alli and Latasha zoomed out of the room. My work of settling them down would have to be repeated later.

Beep, beep, beep was heard coming from the hallway. My admission was coming toward the room and it wasn't ready. I saw the stretcher with a small bundle wrapped in a white quilt lying in the middle and oxygen attached, intravenous (IV) bag hanging, monitor beeping. In the room I scurried about to get Stevie's crib moved to the side so housekeeping, who was late, could move another crib into its space. I looked up as Dr. G stood in the doorway to the room. Alli, Latasha, Dr. G, the transport team, Pat, and most of the other nurses chimed in, "Merry Christmas, Chris!"

Puzzled, I walked toward them as they turned the stretcher around, pulled back the covers and revealed Stevie. The best Christmas present I could have. "He's back!" said Alli excitedly.

I scooped up the little bundle from the cool stretcher and rocked him in the chair Dr. G offered to us. "It was the strangest thing," he said. "He just turned around about 5:30. We didn't think we could get him over here, but we did."

I sat rocking Stevie in the light of the decorated Christmas tree as the rest of the elves worked around us. "Merry Christmas, Stevie," I whispered. "Merry Christmas everyone."

God doesn't need words to hear
He hears the cries of the heart
He listens with His presence
And answers in our hearts

A Fine Spring Day

What a glorious day it was for a picnic. Finally winter was over. Tulips and daffodils pushed out of the cold ground. Through the winter's harsh spell the potential plant had lain silent. The sun's warmth heated the gently flowing breeze and coaxed the stem to break out of the frozen tomb. It stretched to reach the warm sun with half-frozen roots. The bud unfolded and the promise of life was renewed.

It was the first day of spring and children with and without medical compromises would gather and celebrate spring's victory over winter. We would celebrate together our children's lives. Backup electricity for medical equipment had been delivered. A tent had been raised to shelter tender skin. Food, balloons, and face painters were in place. Soon it would be time to get Stevie ready for this glorious day.

Little Stephen and many others live daily with respiratory disorders, their lives compensated and stuck in winter's existence. That winter was no exception.

I had been working in the pediatric rehabilitation unit at Gillette Children's Hospital, Saint Paul. Children would come into our unit to have their braces adjusted, receive therapy; some came because they were chronically disabled and had nowhere else to go.

Stephen had been admitted into our unit following a short stay in a foster home. His foster family couldn't care for him anymore. Stephen was little and he would turn blue quickly if one of his lungs collapsed. He would lie in his crib alone and sometimes cry—a silent, bloodcurdling cry.

The first day he returned to the hospital, he woke up in his new room, looked around, shut his eyes, and for two months didn't respond to anyone.

When he first came to our unit, I had refused to take care of him. He had seemed just too little, too pathetic. I didn't want to hear about the social catastrophes that had brought him into the hospital and I certainly did not want to deal with them. I chose to ignore his silent cry. A few days later, one of Stephen's doctors approached me and said, "I have never known you to walk away from a challenge. Usually you are the one begging for the really 'tough' kids."

~~~

I had earned the reputation of getting too involved with my patients many years earlier. A family had been admitted into the hospital following an airplane accident. I was caring for one of the children, who was in serious condition. His grandmother had died in the crash; his mom, dad and brother clung to life in the intensive care unit. When Jimmy regained consciousness I was elected—actually drafted—to tell him of the loss of his grandmother. "You're the one who spends the most time with him," I was reminded.

I told him and he cried in my arms. Then he wanted to see his mom and dad and brother Mike. Again I was drafted by my co-workers: at the end of my shift, if I wanted to use my own time, I could take Jimmy to see his parents and little brother.

Jimmy and I adjusted the portable equipment around the wheelchair and went to see his Mike. Jimmy looked at him, lying in the bed with tubes and wires everywhere, and said, "Mike is really digging this. He likes flashing lights."

The attending doctor asked him, "Do you have any questions? Do you know how sick he is?"

Jimmy looked at the doctor and said, "Oh yeah, doctor, I know. Last night Mike came and told me he was leaving for heaven to go with grandma. He told me I had to stay here to be with mom and dad. He wasn't crying or anything. I don't know why you still have him hooked up to all this stuff. He's already out of here!"

Then we went to the adult ICU to visit his mom and dad. Later the attending doctor told me that Mike had arrested at midnight the night before. There had been no brain activity since. He had been on life support only until his family could see him.

Two months later, just after Valentine's Day, I helped them arrange a ride home. Jimmy had needed a kidney and a donor had been found in Texas, their home state. His mother and father were in full body casts and Jimmy couldn't sit up yet. They flew back to Texas on my savings account. Before they left the hospital Jimmy gave me a box of candy wrapped in white paper with a red ribbon. The note on the box said, "Thanks for buying me a kidney. Love, Jimmy." It is the most precious box of candy I have ever received.

~~~

Stephen's doctor assigned me to Stephen's care on a one-to-one basis. He said, "If this kid has a chance, you're it. He needs a dose of your craziness."

I took Stephen everywhere. We went to the zoo, out on long walks, and to the stores. We stood in the rain and attended every bingo game the hospital offered. Stephen still didn't respond. Most people thought I was ridiculous. "Why don't you just save your energy and leave him in bed; he doesn't know the difference anyway." Most assumed he was severely mentally challenged or in a chronic vegetative state.

One night, in my rush to finally sit down and chart, I piled medical paraphernalia high on a tray. Everyone in the room was asleep. Ventilators were checked, batteries charging, monitors on, and alarms set. All was finally quiet. Then it happened: I tripped walking to the door. *CRASH!* Monitors beeped, ventilators blared and all the children were awake. The lights went on and nurses rushed in to see what all the ruckus was.

I was at Latasha's bedside when one of the doctors attending Stephen said, "Chris, come quickly. You've got to see this." I ran to Stephen's bedside to find him beet-red in the face. His body was shaking—not from crying or a medical crisis—he was laughing. A *Heheheh* laugh. The loudest laugh you can have through a trach. He even had tears in his eyes. I realized there was a little boy in that bruised shell. Somehow I would find him and coax him out. There was a whole world waiting for him to explore it.

~~~

A time came, however, when we were told Stephen was not expected to live much longer. A major decision needed to be made. Most of his short life had been spent in hospitals. I wanted him to enjoy whatever time he had left in the shelter of a loving home. I wanted Stephen to come live with me, but it was not going to be easy.

Eventually, extensive red tape was cut and neatly placed in a box. Foster care requirements were met, which was something of a feat in itself. I was a single, white girl wanting to take a Native American special-needs child home. I met with

Stephen's biological family and satisfied the requirements of the Indian Child Welfare Act. Social Services met with my family, friends and co-workers, and determined that I was a "stable human being."

An inventory of needed supplies had to be taken, items ordered and delivered. Oxygen, IV supplies, medicine, and other ancillary services were contracted; and needed equipment arrived. Requirements for public-aid and waivered services were met. Nursing services were interviewed, one selected and start-up nurses were hired to care for Stephen. Protocols, policies and treatments were written and learned. Home-care physicians were contacted, evaluations completed and follow-up appointments scheduled. Home modifications were made. Everything needed was in place—except the pivotal nursing care. I needed to hire one more full-time nurse before Stephen could come home.

Wintertime in hospitals is long and difficult. Viruses rampantly invade the air. Many people struggle for life in the surrounding rooms. Stephen had contracted one of these hospital invaders; consequently my dream of our being home together had to be postponed. His body weak and his system too compensated, a flu shot was determined to be "not worth the risk." Stephen was gravely ill. The medical professionals encouraged me to rethink my decision to bring him into my life at home.

This further hindered my ability to hire another nurse for Stephen, as "it isn't a good business decision to invest in someone who's going to die" and "nurses don't want to get involved with a child who is going to die. It's just too hard."

As far as I was concerned, he had already entered my heart. I wanted Stephen to know that there was one person in this world who loved him, no matter what. I spent my on- and off - duty time with him. Later I would learn that caring for the dying is not a choice but a calling.

Stephen's lung disease and type-A influenza engineered a deadly combination. He struggled to breathe and fever was a constant companion. One day, his airways collapsed. He turned an upsetting shade of blue. Nurses, doctors, therapists huddled around his bed and worked frantically trying to ease his breathing and fever. Then my head nurse said, "Chris, I'm sorry—we are losing him." The most advanced medical interventions had not been able to remedy Stephen's airway collapse.

I clamped his tubes, disconnected others and scooped him into my arms. I ran into the bathroom, slipped down to the floor using the wall to guide me, held him in my lap, and sang "Jesus loves me . . ." in the dark.

No bright lights, no hustle and bustle, just quiet love. Stephen shouldn't have to live in the hospital, I felt, and he shouldn't have to die there either. The bathroom floor had been the closest thing available.

Miraculously Stephen exhaled a big sigh; he was breathing again. I kicked open the bathroom door. One of the nurses rushed in and shouted, "He's alive!" She grabbed him and placed him back in his crib. There the doctors and nurses huddled again and worked in the artificial light hooking him back up to his many tubes and wires. The baby eagle had survived his brush with death.

Over and over again that dance of wait repeats itself. The promise of new life breaks through the cold ground in the spring. The plant is given its first drink by the falling rain as it stretches heavenward. My Stephen reached for life and heaven came down to meet him.

Weeks later, at the completion of a forty-day prayer vigil led by my mom, Stephen was going home. Home nursing was finally in place. My licensing social worker, who had become my comrade, escorted us out of the hospital. Some months previous she had left a business card by Stephen's bed. On the back she had written, "Anyone interested in Stephen, call me." Now she would witness one of the most controversial home-goings the hospital had ever experienced.

Stephen wore a new outfit that had been presented to us at a "new mom-new son" shower. The shower had been given for us by one of Stephen's "roomies" and a good friend. We enjoyed cake, presents and well wishes. God's blessings escorted us out of the hospital that day.

Stephen had lost a lot of weight due to this "flu" so I wrapped his fragile skin in a blanket. The ride home was short in comparison to the weeks of preparation and waiting. At my house, Stephen's room had windows from the ceiling to the floor on three sides. It was decorated with a border of balloons, and small stuffed animals sat perched on the curtain rods. The room glowed with sunlight. I felt like a new mom as I laid him in his new crib for the first time. I had been given a special boy and I was very thankful.

I reveled in that thought only a short time before a piece of medical equipment needed attention. Supplies and medical equipment filled every available space. Therapy balls, bolsters, switch-adapted toys spilled out from the closets. Social workers, foster-care agency workers, therapists, pharmacists, teachers, nurses, and vendors invaded our privacy. I struggled to keep a sense of normalcy and a place of peace.

Stephen slept, a sweet uninterrupted sleep. He stopped losing weight and slowly began to regain his strength. His cares occupied most of the available time. For weeks Stephen's body had shuddered when he was touched. He resisted physical contact, making his many cares a creative challenge. Patterning and repetition slowly transmitted sentiments of security to his bruised emotions.

One morning as I gave him a bath, he reached out and touched my arm with his hand. I didn't move. That was the first time Stephen had touched my arm without quickly withdrawing it. Tears came to my eyes as I thought that maybe he trusted me. He continued to grow and gain weight. Stephen had miraculously survived his siege of influenza.

When that influenza ended, pertussis began. "The risk is greater than the possibility of contracting the disease." So Stephen had not been vaccinated for whooping cough. He started coughing and couldn't stop.

In the Emergency Room we were assisted by one of my former co-workers. He thought something was caught in Stephen's airway, so an emergency bronchoscopy was performed. Stephen's doctor numbed Stephen's throat and inserted a tiny fibro-optic scope through his trach tube. When Stephen was three months old, a small tube had been placed in his trachea to assist his breathing and allow secretion evacuation, as well as augmented oxygen supply directly to his lungs.

The doctor looked through the eyepiece into Stephen's tube and said, "Wow! Look at this. If I'm right, we're looking at pertussis." I saw swollen, red, weepy airways. He quickly instructed me about how to hold the scope and rushed out of the room to retrieve his colleagues.

The role of mom and nurse was a difficult status to master, a double-edged sword of familiarity versus professionalism that was new to me. Stephen's doctor returned to the room looking sheepish. He entered saying, "Chris, I'm sorry. I forgot you were Stephen's mom, not my nurse." I accepted his apology and affirmed his zeal. He left again returning with many colleagues who were fascinated to see "pertussis firsthand." Stephen had taught class that day.

We returned home. We cared for Stephen by focusing on clearing his lungs. Then, before his coughs became violent, he would be sedated. This cycle continued for ten days until the disease began to subside. One morning I heard a loud raspy noise and hurried to Stephen's room. Stephen lay asleep in his bed. His muscles were relaxed, his breathing steady and rhythmic, and a smile graced his face. He was laughing. Stephen was laughing, with pertussis.

He had survived the winter and its bedfellows, the viruses. It was time to wake Stephen and put on his brand-new outfit for our spring celebration. He was sleeping later then usual. One of his monitors signaled that he was awake. I entered his room, excited to get on with the day, and saw a little boy working hard to breathe and appearing slightly blue. This picture did not fit the day's plans.

I wished I could turn the page and start the day over again ending with a different conclusion. Stephen was not breathing well. I grabbed the ambu, a soft bag used to gently blow air into the lungs, simulating breathing. I began breathing with him this way, increasing his air exchange. His color improved.

This wasn't supposed to happen, especially not today.

Stephen's lung sounds revealed increased fluid; his body was warm with fever. We were not going anywhere. The doctor was called, antibiotics were started and Stephen went comfortably back to sleep. When the sun began to set and the spring celebration was over, Stephen woke up feeling a bit better. I opened the windows, painted a smiley face on his cheek and ate dinner in his room on the floor. He was happy.

When the nurse came in to take over Stephen's care, she asked, "How was the picnic? How was the celebration?"

I simply replied, "We missed it. We missed the first day of spring." When report was finished, I slouched down into the rocking chair and rocked myself to sleep.

~~~

Before long, it was the beginning of fall. Stephen and I were going for an evening walk. The air was crisp. Stephen laughed as the wheelchair rolled over the fallen red and orange leaves, making a rustling crackle. Our evening's walk took us to a baseball park. I parked Stephen's wheelchair by the high fence behind home plate. A group of young people moved away to the other side of the bleachers as we approached.

The batter swung and missed. The next throw was hit with the bat, creating a loud crack. Stephen laughed. Another hit. *Clunk.* Stephen laughed again. A big *Heheee* laugh. He laughed with his whole body as the hits kept coming. Watching him laugh, I laughed and before I knew it I was lying on the ground next to the wheelchair laughing uncontrollably.

I opened my eyes to see one of the young men who had walked away from us before, standing over me. "What are you laughing for, lady? There is nothing funny here."

Before I could answer he walked out onto the field and

talked with the pitcher. The team huddled. Maybe they would ask us to leave. That had happened before; we had been places and people had told us to "get out of here."

The pitcher walked over to us with the other young man and asked if Stephen would like to hear another hit. Upon my request, he asked Stephen himself and Stephen responded with his sign, "Yes." The pitcher went back to the mound and threw another ball. *Clunk!* And then another. *Clunk!* And then another. *Clunk!* Soon all the people in the surrounding bleachers were standing, sitting, doubled-over laughing around Stephen. When no one could laugh any more, the "game" was over.

The pitcher walked with us out of the park and across the street through the falling leaves. He paused to give Stephen a "high-five"—a special handshake. Then shaking my hand the usual way, he said, "Today is just like the first day of spring. Just like the first day of spring."

Stephen and I smiled our secret to each other. We hadn't missed anything after all.

Sweat Lodge Prayer

The light of the Great Spirit surrounds us,

The love of Wakan Tanka enfolds us.

The power of the Creator protects us.

The presence of God watches over us.

Wherever I am, the Great Spirit is.

Told to me by Auntie Valerie during
the Blessing of the Wind ceremony

Blessing of the Wind

The American Indian elders sat on the floor by Stephen's hospital bed. I jabbered about all of Stephen's little details. They listened and said very little. I explained about his life in the hospital and my progress in obtaining a foster-care license. Much of the time they just listened and nodded. The day was especially busy in the rehabilitation unit and they didn't seem to mind my walking in and out of the room performing ancillary nursing duties.

When nighttime came and Stephen and the other children in the room were tucked into bed, the younger of the three men gave me a picture. He explained who each was; all were Stephen's ancestors. Then he presented me with a wooden flute and said, "You will get your strength from the wind as you learn to walk upon it. I give you this flute to honor you. The wind needed to make it sing is the same wind that will give you courage to carry this baby eagle. The wind will be your guide."

The oldest Indian man reached in his front pocket and gave me a pipe. He said, "As you care for this wounded eagle, he will teach you the ways of the Great Spirit. Hold this pipe and give it to its owner." They handed it to me and left.

I stood in Stephen's hospital room and held the objects close to my heart. I didn't know what they meant, but I felt honored and thankful to hold them.

The next day, Stephen's Auntie Valerie came to visit him in the hospital. I was excited to tell her about my visit with the elders. She stayed with Stephen for a time, while I caught up with my hospital duties. During my break, I sat next to Auntie Valerie, who had become my good friend, and told her of my visitors the night before.

She was astounded. She asked me what they looked like and how they talked. I told her everything I could remember. She just kept shaking her head. When she asked me what I did, she laughed as I told her that I told them about everything! I had learned that most of the time Native Americans speak very little. Not me; I love to talk.

Then I showed Auntie Valerie the picture. She took it in her hands and cradled it to her heart, as one would when a lost child returns. She asked if she could keep it and I nodded yes. Then she turned, kissed Stephen and walked out. I had no idea what she thought about my encounter or the picture.

A few months later when Stephen and I were home together, she came to visit. This visit she brought the picture the Indian man had given me, and a scrapbook. She opened it and told me all about her family. She turned one of the pages and pointed to an empty space. She took the picture the elder had given me and it fit perfectly in the discolored spot in the scrapbook.

I looked at her and she explained, "My uncle gave this picture to my father before my grandfather died. He buried it with my grandfather. I called everyone. No one had another copy and no one had seen the picture again until you got it." She looked at me with tenderness and compassion, and said, "My grandfather visited you." I told her I was speechless. She laughed and said, "That's a first."

A couple of months later when Stephen got sick, I called for one of the medicine men to come and bless him. I wanted

Stephen to be saturated in his cultural ancestry and, instead, it covered me with its purity and beauty.

The medicine man came to our home. He prayed with us and played his drum. Stephen loved the sound of the drum. When he was done playing, he set the drum down. I got the pipe I had been given and handed it to him. Auntie Valerie, who was there too, smiled and walked over to where I held Stephen. She and the medicine man stood side by side in front of me.

She took the pipe in her hand and said, "As my grandfather has honored you, so do I. I give you my sister's son. May the wind rise to meet you and may you rest comfortably in the shelter it provides."

Then the medicine man spoke. "Stephen was named in his mother's womb, 'Eagle Spirit.' He will fly as high as an eagle but on the wings of another." He and Auntie Valerie each held the pipe in their open hands as the medicine man said, "Your name, Windwalker, is Child's Warrior Woman." He took some tobacco from his pouch, crushed it into a fine dust and made a line on Stephen's forehead, then on mine.

"As the arrow flies, so will you," he continued.

I held Stephen in my arms, not sure what had just transpired. Auntie Valerie kissed Stephen and said as she left, "May the blessing of the wind that you received tonight sustain and keep you."

They come to us needy, yet ask for nothing
They watch us with their souls, yet they have no eyes
They reach for us with treasures, yet they own nothing
They teach us with their life, and ask nothing in return

CLN

Franny's Family

I sat on the exercise mat on the floor in Stephen's room. This was the easiest way to help Stephen stretch. Lots of hours every day were spent stretching and ranging his tight muscles. Range of motion exercises were developed by his physical therapists and performed five or six times every day.

Today Auntie Valerie joined us. She visited Stephen every chance she had and it was heartwarming to see Stephen respond to her. We enjoyed the stories she told us about her family. Her sister Franny was Stephen's mother.

Auntie Valerie described Franny as tall and husky, with a low, steady tone. She commanded attention with her presence. Valerie and Franny had been raised between Minneapolis' inner city and a South Dakota Indian reservation, their homeland. Stephen's entrance into this world brought him into a clash of those cultures.

Auntie Valerie told the story this way.

Stephen had been born prematurely; his weight was just a little over two pounds at birth and without invitation, dangling tubes and wires immediately intruded their lives. The sterile hospital environment, with its incessant noise of machines, was worlds apart from the serene buffalo lands of her origin. Franny could find no comfort for herself or for her baby in the neonatal ICU at Metropolitan Medical Center, Minneapolis.

Her precious child, the dream of her heart, lay quietly encircled by bright lights in a metal, temperature-controlled box. Small patches covered his eyes, needles pierced his arms and legs, a small tube blew oxygen into his nose. Gloved hands stemming from gloved bodies penetrated the portholes of his new house. He lay quietly. A short time ago this little life had rested comfortably in her womb. They had shared the same heartbeat and were constantly aware of each other's presence.

Now she had to cross over into his world by covering her comfortable sweats with a hospital gown. She felt as if she had landed on the wrong planet. She had been reading books about baby growth and development. This premature birth had not been in her plans.

She reached in through the portholes of Stephen's metal house and touched him for the first time outside of her own body. By a force not of this world, not of this time, the gloves she wore melted. The bright lights dimmed and the blaring alarms were replaced by distant drumbeats and memories. With their hands joined, she realized they were still one. Stephen moved his head and opened his fingers. The monitor showed a slower, more steady heartbeat. His breathing eased. Senseless guilt and tears ended as she heard her child's soul.

During the next few weeks Stephen made some progress. He grew and slowly gained weight. His quiet and somewhat shy demeanor had covered an obstinate personality that helped him survive the many medical complications that arose from his premature birth.

Seemingly countless times, Franny had sat with the medical planners of his care, struggling to comprehend. Lonely nights were spent pacing the floor, wondering if they would share another sunrise.

Baby showers and homecoming hot dishes were replaced with isolation and unending explanations of what went wrong.

Baby books were replaced with medical journals. Nursery furniture was moved to accommodate awkward medical equipment. Baby announcements were replaced with lengthy financial forms. Soon she would bring Stephen home. A different beginning than they had planned, but a beginning.

She kissed him goodbye and left to visit her parents' home. Traveling to the place of her childhood, she would ask for her family's blessing. She hoped to return with her ancestors' wisdom and her grandfather's tenacious determination.

Upon reaching the reservation, she learned that she would be honored by her father in a vision quest. During this time in the wilderness, she would gather the wisdom that she would need to care for her small son.

Sleepless nights surrounded by cold hospital walls gave way to starry nights and radiant sunny days. Her strength was restored. Her constant companion on the vision quest was a brown buffalo. They walked together. Franny's new companion protected her from any perils and she rested in his strength and warmth. Her ancestors were ever-present and through the fire's smoke she saw the many guides that had helped her along life's red path. She lingered in their glow as they acknowledged and respected the path she had chosen. She heard her son's breath in the oak tree's whisper and she saw him run on the moonbeams. She heard him call her name in the crackle of the fire. She was ready to return to her son; she had all she needed to continue her journey.

Franny returned to the hospital with arms full of blankets and baskets of food. She hurried to her son's room and stopped abruptly. "Where is Stephen?! Where is my son?!"

A nurse heard her scream and ran to her side. "He's been

moved," the nurse said, as she led her to his new room. She entered with happiness in her heart. "Stephen, I am so happy to see . . .." The blankets fell out of her arms, the basket dropped and food spread over the floor. Franny ran from the hospital.

Stephen lay in his hospital bed that he now shared with two new bed partners: one, a tube through a hole in his throat into his trachea to supply oxygen to his collapsing lungs, and the other a small tube inserted directly into his stomach to provide formula. They were to be his companions for life. The attaching tubes and wires lay loosely on his bed.

He felt much better than he had a couple of weeks earlier when pneumonia had invaded his life. Contact with Franny's family had been attempted, but unsuccessful. Emergency intervention had occurred when Stephen's life was believed to have been in danger.

Now, hospital personnel tried to find Franny again.

Two weeks passed and Franny was found dead. She lay lifeless next to a message that she had written with her own blood. It said, "I have gone to be with my son."

Franny believed, as do many others, that when a hole is cut in your body, your soul leaves. In Native American tradition, blessings of purification and encompassing safety were offered prior to the time that a battle was fought. In that way, if the shell of one's soul were broken, one's spirit would remain. Stephen had not yet had this blessing and, in Franny's heart, she felt he was gone. She would now travel to another spirit world to be reunited with him. She was prepared for her journey.

Many times, cultural integrity and medical management clash. The struggle depletes energy from all involved, leaving the person or ideal for which they fought isolated. The isolation further compromises the intended recipient. Families who struggle with life's unfairness become the unfortunate recipients of some of life's most stringent rules. The resulting compromise of one's moral standards to accommodate system limits, instead of nurturing, destroys.

I will care for you
I know the stars by name
Not a tear falls that does not touch Me
Every being breathes My life
I will care for you
I will provide for you
I asked you to follow me and you have
As the plane soars above the stormy ground
As it leaves behind the clouds
And climbs above the darkness
You sup with me
You stay by my side
I will provide for you
The limits of this world will not hurt you
Remember the sun
The source of light itself will touch you
You will live within it
You will find joy above the clouds
Come with me
The road to the throne is easy in the light
You are my lamb
I care for you
See through the tears
I am here
Take the children with you
And lead them to me with love
They will greet you
They will strengthen you
Through their pain
I will comfort them
As an anvil, as a harp
You will ease their fear
This world sheds tears for the children
For they are their own
But only a few hear them drop
As a cymbal their tears split your solace
You can hear their tears
Walk carefully beside Me
Their tears are Mine
You have heard the silent cries
You listen with My ears   CLN

Cabin by the Lake

Stephen had come home in March of 1989. Our first weeks outside hospital walls were spent learning how to juggle medical necessities and daily desires. Stephen was not expected to live very long, so many days and nights were spent with very little nursing help. Stephen learned that touch was pleasant and that someone would be there to meet his needs. Everything was new for him. He learned that the sun coming up in the morning was a time to be active, and when darkness covered the Earth, quiet time followed. The phone's ring would startle him, until he understood that a fun voice followed the ring. Every breeze, every shadow, every sound brought him to full attention. His medical interventions became routine. More nurses joined his "in-home force" as he survived frequent medical crises.

In the summer, Stephen and I took our first trip to Wisconsin to meet grandma and grandpa. My parents had been supportive of my decision to take Stephen home with me, but they also wondered "why a single girl like you would want to take on such a hard kid."

Arriving at my mom and dad's house, I carried little Stephen in and laid him on the couch. My dad followed me to the truck and helped me unload the medical equipment and supplies needed for our two-day visit. My mom sat next to Stephen on the couch, afraid to touch him. "I don't want to hurt him. I don't know where to touch him."

After arranging everything in their small cottage by the

lake, I held Stephen in my arms. Dad had told mom that he would build a house for her, and he had. Not only did they nail the boards, paint and varnish, dad also had cut down the trees and made a sawmill out of broken parts. They did the whole thing.

Mom made us a cup of tea and time passed as it had during previous visits with the exception of the *Sssssssshhhhhh* noise of oxygen and occasional monitor beep. Dad commented that with all Stephen's stuff, the living room resembled a hospital room instead of his house. He said, "I guess I'll have to put up with it, because you're going to do what you want anyway."

As he mumbled about my stubbornness, mom quipped, "She gets that from you, Lyle."

Later, when mom was making supper, dad said, "Bringing that boy home to live with you isn't the first thing you've done a little risky."

Growing up on a farm in Wisconsin, I became close to the animals. I would sit and hold sick animals rather than play with my friends. My closest companion was a black lamb named Jezebel. One of my chores was to bring the cows in from the field for milking in the evening. I would hike up to the field, sometimes stopping by a big puddle to fish with a bare branch for awhile, and then lead the cows back to the barn. I'd take the cowbell off the lead cow's neck and put it around mine. The cows would follow me down to the barn and I'd talk to them the whole time, telling them all about my day in school. Most of the time my stories would continue while my dad milked my friends. He laughed as he remembered some of my tales.

Dad reminded me, too, about the Famous Rodeo Day. Helping mom and dad during harvest time one year earned me a trip to a small local rodeo with my dad. I was very excited to see the animals, especially the cows. I was horrified when one of the mean cowboys placed a rope around a baby calf and threw him on the ground.

I asked my dad for some money to get a hot dog. He obliged. After much begging he finally allowed me to go to the stand all by myself. My dad could watch me the entire time. The bulls were out in the arena and I saw that they had captured his attention. When I arrived at the hot dog stand, I slipped away to the back of the stalls. I walked past many adults to the calf pens. I opened the gate and clanked on the fence so calves would run out. They did.

When the cowboys saw the calves out of their pens, they chased after them—so I opened the gate to the cow pens, too. That day no more cows or baby calves would be hurt.

I hurried back to the stand, got my hot dog and took my place in the bleachers next to my dad.

"How's the hot dog?" he asked.

"Good," I replied. No other words were exchanged between us about the pens.

We arrived home earlier than expected. When mom asked why, dad smiled at me and just said, "The cows got out."

Then mom chimed in with the Deer Hunting Saga. My dad had allowed me to go hunting with him one year. Many people on farms hunt to provide food for their families during the long, cold Wisconsin winters. It was the last day of deer-hunting season. Tensions mounted as the sun began to sink lower and lower in the sky. Not one person that my dad hunted with had his deer yet. Soon the season would end.

I enjoyed walking quietly through the woods. Sometimes

my excitement about a toad or pheasant brought others to bois-
terous laughter. Each time we were quickly shushed and the
appropriate "hunting silence" was regained. On this day we
had had a picnic on top of a big hill. The air was crisp and
clean. The sun dropping in the sky was a beautiful ending to a
beautiful day.

Suddenly about sunset, one of the group whispered, "Deer,
eleven o'clock." I immediately dropped to my knees as previously instructed. Then I saw them—the most graceful creatures
imaginable, frolicking in a field of flowers just ahead of us. Two
large deer and two small deer jumped and played in the tall
grass. I looked back at my dad to make sure he saw this beautiful picture, but he had the gun up to his eye. At first I thought
he was doing that to get a better look at them. When someone
whispered, "Get ready. Aim," I realized that they were going to
shoot and kill the deer.

I sprang up from my knees and ran out in front of the rifled
men shouting, "Run, deer, run!" They did. All of them.

The ride home was very long and very quiet. No one said a
word. My dad didn't invite me hunting with him anymore.

Cuddling Stephen in my arms, I reminded dad of the rides
he gave mom in his old Indian Chief motorcycle with a sidecar.
He got the bike in pieces and not one of his friends thought he
would get it together. He did. He restored it to its pre-crash
state and gave my mom rides we'll never forget.

Mom said, "I trusted you. You promised you'd be careful."
Dad pointed out that mom was still alive, and the story continued. Dad had started out slowly, but soon mom was flying in
the sidecar. He hung the car over ditches and off the sides of
bridges. Mom didn't care to get on the bike again for a long

time after that ride.

My older brother did, though. Mom was looking out the window one morning and saw the sidecar going on one side of the clothesline and dad on the motorcycle on the other side of the pole. No one was hurt as the cotter pin that connected the sidecar and the bike had rattled loose.

Laughter filled the cottage and somewhere in the happy memories Stephen's medical equipment faded into the sunset. Soon mom held Stephen in the rocking chair and sang a familiar "Jesus loves me . . .." She held him and rocked him for hours. Stephen enjoyed the different sounds of the wind in the pine trees and the waves lapping the lakeshore.

The next morning at breakfast, dad looked at me as he had when I'd let the cows out. He smiled and said, "I always wished you'd settle down with a man. I just hoped it was one out of diapers!"

When I began to pack Stephen's medical stuff in the truck that evening, I returned to the cabin to see a tender scene. Stephen lay on his white quilt in the middle of the couch. Behind him the sparkling lake was visible through two big picture windows. Kneeling down in front of the couch was my dad. His hand rested on Stephen's small shoulder. Mom sat at Stephen's feet. One of her hands was on my father's hand on Stephen's shoulder, and her other hand on her heart. I overheard one of them say, "You're a lucky little boy. She's one of the best. You've got a good mom."

I stepped back outside, thanked God for such wonderful parents and confidently walked back in.

Yes, pretend it is still night,
and you are standing outside
the tent, looking at the sky,
and you feel it:

the stars want to come to you.

When days feel thick,
this is the presence of the angels.

Kate Christianson

Tommy's First Christmas

Tonight I watched my friend hold her son while he died. The cessation of his life was expected, yet unannounced. Many hours of counsel, days of prayer and months of care did not prepare my friend for the final slicing of her son's breath. She held him and spoke soothing, gentle words expressing her love for him. At her request I remained in the room as they exchanged their last words. She looked at little Tommy and said with authority, "The angels are here. They want to play with you now. They will take care of you."

Glancing over at me through tear-filled eyes she said, "Tommy, Chris will help me. I will be okay." She kissed him tenderly on his cheek and he died.

Grief is not kind enough to kill. Tommy rested in angel arms and my friend shuddered. She had walked in the valley of the shadow of death as her precious newborn withered away. The valley had consumed her.

She tried to continue to be a part of the world that took her son. She sought to believe that death's painful separation was in accordance with God's plan. Learning to run with rocks in your shoes is treacherous. The feeling of lost dreams does not stop when the funeral is over. Nor does it stop when weeks or years go by. Change is painful. Holidays, birthdays, anniversaries, the first day of school, summer camp, graduations, weddings—nothing is ever the same again.

The inhabitants of this world exist every day determined to leave legacies that are the accumulation of their breath—

awards, medals of honor, financial strongholds, and political empires. Entire lifetimes are spent hoping one's memory will continue beyond one's physical body. We are outsiders living in the shadow of memories on this Earth.

I had been introduced to Tommy's mother in the Intensive Care Unit at Saint Paul Children's Hospital. Stephen and Tommy shared a room. Both of them were hospitalized with RSV (respiratory syncytial virus). It was just after Christmastime in 1989. As we comforted our sons, we found solace in each other's company. Our fresh relationship knew no boundaries. Differences of race, culture, age, personal morals, religion did not exist in our children's struggle. The armor we wore to guard our souls and protect our rights was quickly shed. We found comfort together in our sorrow. Grief was our unwelcome companion.

One night we made our beds in the chairs next to our sons' cribs and reminisced about the Christmas holiday just past.

Stephen had been sick that Christmas. He struggled to breathe. His tiny airways had collapsed with the heavy secretions that clung to their sides. The cords that make the airway strong hadn't developed due to his prematurity. His respiratory rate increased as his body craved oxygen. The oxygen pumped into his trachea wasn't reaching its intended destination due to the frequent airway collapses. Every time he coughed they would collapse again, creating a dangerous downward cycle.

Sitting in the doctor's office on Christmas Eve morning, we were both struggling. Stephen struggled to breathe and I struggled with the reality before me. Stephen was sick for Christmas.

Dr. M sat and talked with me. He knew the frustrations and accomplishments we had shared the last nine months. "I'm sorry he's so sick, Chris. We can put him in the hospital and do our best to help him through this crisis, but I don't know if it will help or not." He held my hand as he talked about the "progression of his lung disease."

Then he said, "Why don't you take him home and give him the Christmas you talked about last year. No matter what the outcome, you will always have this Christmas to remember."

We would share our first Christmas together out of the hospital. Stephen remained very sick, but was a part of all the festivities at my parents' house. Hours were spent preparing for this special holiday. Even Stephen's medical equipment was decorated. And outside, fresh snow blanketed the fields and glistened like thousands of dancing fireflies. Ice freezing on the lake groaned deeply and snow crunched underfoot. The holiday season was filled with friends and family bearing wishes of holiday joy. We felt like a part of the "real" world.

Stephen lay on my lap that Christmas Eve. My brothers and sisters and their families accepted us. With every breath Stephen took, I breathed in the miracle of this Christmas.

Stephen smiled when my nephews and nieces sang Happy Birthday to baby Jesus, while mom lit the candles on a small cake. I held Stephen in my arms as we rode out of the sparkling snow and into the city lights.

Stephen's respiratory status continued to decline, so we had sought refuge in Dr. M's hospital. That's where I had met Tommy's mom. Our hearts merged together surrounded by a common emotion. Grief flows in like the tide, sweeps over you, saturating every cell, then leaves again. Those who grieve are linked to one another.

I would go the next day with her to make funeral arrangements for Tommy. But this night, she chose to stay in the hospital with Stephen and me. She stayed as our friend. "ICU sleep" is another good oxymoron; healing rest does not come easily within the walls of the busy unit.

This night, Tommy's mom held Stephen's hand. "I want to hold onto someone who knows where my Tommy is," she said. "Stephen knows."

My fitful sleep was interrupted by the third part of a recurring dream. Tommy's mom and I sat facing each other as I shook, telling her what I had just dreamt. Weeks earlier I had had a dream: I was walking in a field of wildflowers. The air was crisp and cool and many flocks of ducks were migrating overhead. I came upon two bare trees. They stood about eight feet apart from each other and were the same height. Toward the top third of the trees was a wide flat branch like the horizontal bar on a cross. On top of that branch, Stephen lay lifeless, wrapped in a white quilt. I woke from that dream sobbing and trembling.

About a week after that, I woke in the middle of the night after another dream. I had seen the same field of wildflowers. I heard the same migrating ducks overhead, saw the same trees standing parallel to each other. As I approached the trees this time, I saw my Stephen lying on the cross branch wrapped in a white quilt. Underneath him, I sat—alive, but pinned to the ground by a long spear through my body. The edges of his quilt danced with the wind as it flowed around us. I woke from that dream with the same intense awareness I had felt after the last dream. I trembled for a long time.

And on this night, the dream had visited me a third time. I saw the wildflowers, heard the migrating birds, felt the cool, crisp air blowing around us. I saw Stephen wrapped in a white quilt on a wide branch between two trees. Underneath, I saw myself pierced by the long spear.

This time, I also saw a white, fuzzy substance flowing from our bodies. Stephen's white fog met with my white fog above the tallest tree. When they met, they merged into a continuous white fuzzy stream. On the wind, I held Stephen's hand and effortlessly we walked together. I looked down at the two trees that still held my son, myself still stuck to the ground.

The part of me that cared for Stephen was dying. Terrific pain was evident in this separation. Stephen's body lay quietly, just a shell, no longer needed. The white fuzzy substance was the wind, the breath of God. Our bodies had been created for this joining, this time. For eternity we would ride on the wings of God.

Tommy's mom and I held each other a long time in the presence of the precious gift we had been given. She stood up and said, "I am going home now. I understand why I hurt. Like you I was called to be a horse for awhile. That horse is dying now. My soul joined with Tommy's a long time ago for eternity.

"Good night, Windwalker," she said as she left. "Have a good ride."

Most people measure their happiness in terms of physical pleasure and possession. If happiness is to be so measured, I who cannot hear nor see, have every reason to sit in a corner with folded hands and weep. But as sinners sometimes stand up in a meeting to testify to the goodness of God, so one who is called afflicted may rise up in gladness to testify of His goodness.

The struggle of life is one of our greatest blessings. It makes us patient, sensitive, and Godlike. It teaches us that, although the world is full of suffering, it is also full of the overcoming of it.

Helen Keller

Dr. J and the Miracle

I sat in the Pediatric Intensive Care Unit in Saint Paul, confused and disappointed that Stephen had been admitted to the hospital. We had weathered many compromising medical crises at home. Some medical experts and coordinators felt Stephen should be cared for in the hospital whenever he became sick. A cold could easily turn into pneumonia, and a seizure often required IV intervention. Infections that most of us can fight as we go about our daily routines, often stop the chronically ill right in their tracks.

We had found in the last three years, however, that Stephen recovered more quickly and with fewer complications when he was cared for at home. The caregivers who came into our home got to know Stephen. They learned his cares and understood his personality. This created an environment where he could heal and grow comfortably. It also was far less stressful for me. Orienting the nurses to Stephen's many medical cares took hours. Understanding his awkward sign language and eye-pointing techniques took days to master. Stephen needed an interpreter during his hospital stays, as his audible voice remained silent. The nurses did not have time to learn his intricate communication system, yet they needed his input to determine his level of pain or comfort. Time was a necessary commodity and communication an asset for recovery. I knew Stephen's silent language—it spoke loudly to me.

Nursing care had changed drastically since the time that I had begun to practice. Years ago, one nurse cared for three or four ill people in the hospital by personally accessing them and treating them. Now, it seemed that care was chopped into separate categories and delivered by many different people. The topic of reports and in-services often centered around "caring for the whole patient." Separate categories, different caregivers, and treat the whole patient? It had become difficult.

We had chosen home care and been blessed to find good nursing and ancillary services. Nurses came in all sizes and shapes. They arrived at our house with different backgrounds, cultures, religions, political views, and lifestyles. Sometimes care was hindered by these differences, but most often Stephen's needs bridged the gap of diversity. I was thankful for each caregiver and service that cared for Stephen.

I had hoped that it would be only a matter of hours until we could return home. Stephen had been uncomfortable with a stomachache and I had that "feeling" that something dreadful was happening to his body. He continued to laugh and smile, but he hurt. Five weeks later we sat in the Surgical Waiting Room, still in the hospital.

"Come in please, come in. There is room for all of you. Squeeze in a little tighter. Good morning, Chris," the distinguished doctor said. It was time for rounds at Children's Hospital. The eager residents followed their superior closely, striving to hear every word. It wasn't often the residents were able to work with a visiting specialist of this caliber. They quickly entered the small Surgical Waiting Room, like grade-school children after recess.

The smell of shampoo was still evident as they filed in. The hospital's sterile odor had not yet adhered to their clothing. Ladies with newly-applied makeup and clean-shaven gentlemen stood close to me in the room.

It was a refreshing sight after being up most of the night talking with residents who had worked the last twenty-four hours without a shower. The group of residents stood at attention, propping open the heavy fire door that separated surgery from the intensive care unit. Dr. J stood with his black suspenders and Mickey Mouse tie directly in front of me.

"Okay, let's get down to business," he announced. "Today I would like to share with you a case that has interested me for the last several weeks. Please pay close attention, as we will discuss this only once. This is a case of misfortune. A six-year-old boy with multiple medical handicaps was treated with depakane to assist in seizure control. He presented with difficulty handling feedings, stomach discomfort and an increase in seizure activity. He was admitted to the ICU with dehydration and ascites. His lab values are here." Passing them out to the attentive residents, he said, "Review them quickly and we will discuss them."

Stephen and I sat, feeling quite out of place. We had been preparing for surgery since 5 a.m. The intensive care unit was busy with morning rounds, morning cares. Technicians announced, "Shooting," as they took ordered x-rays. Other technicians obtained blood from lines inserted in children. The smell of fresh coffee mingled with fresh soap, smothering the sick smells that lingered from night's war of survival. Mothers, fathers and caregivers exchanged greetings as they left their loved one's side for a short hour while the doctors and nurses made their private morning rounds. We uttered prayers of comfort for our children as we departed from their rooms, creating a mass exodus. We met in the hall of the ICU. Our paths brushed each morning at this time. Exchanging nods instead of how-do-you-do's, we hid our stale breath.

In one hour we would be back at our battle stations. Shortly we would file back into the ICU through the same door and return to our posts. It would be another day before we would see each other again.

Stephen and I had been escorted to the Surgical Waiting Room this morning. Instead of rounds at the bedside, medical rounds were now being held in our presence in the room where we waited together for surgery. Dr. J's voice interrupted. "Okay, who would like to evaluate these lab orders?"

Eager hands shot up, hoping for approval from the respected doctor.

"Okay, you there in the back. Have a crack at it."

A tall, thin, dark-haired young resident cleared his throat as if to begin an oration on the laboratory values that he held before him. "This child is in trouble," he said. "That is, if he is still alive. He has very little if any fibrinogen in his blood. His blood has no clotting capacity. Therefore he will, or has, died."

Dr. J asked, "Can anyone tell me how this child could survive? Any one at all?" No one answered.

"Okay, let's look at these lab results." He handed out another stack of papers that were quickly passed person to person.

"Anyone?" A pretty young lady raised her hand, hoping to be asked to continue this exploration of values. Her brown freckles hid her quick blush as she was called upon. "These values show overwhelming sepsis—origin unknown."

"How would we treat this infection?" queried Dr. J. "Okay, speak up." Many voices now intermingled, creating the effect common during a press conference. Stephen rested in my arms while the exchange of information continued.

"The outcome?"

"Death," one of the residents stated matter-of-factly.

"Explain, please."

Dr. J waited as the blond, suntanned resident continued. "The organism has infected the blood. The antibiotics are not stopping the infection. The increased volume of fluid has caused congestive heart failure that makes the heart pump more fluid than the lungs are able to handle, and the blood cannot clot. Therefore, a major bleed would result, terminating life." He ended his case as a lawyer standing contentedly before a judge. "Simply stated, this child had one too many strikes against him."

"Anyone else?" The residents only nodded in agreement with their colleague.

Dr. J then turned and faced me. He knelt down on his right knee and removed his dark glasses, putting them into his top pocket. He placed his hand on Stephen and looked directly into my eyes.

"Class, meet Stephen and his mom."

Bewildered, the residents looked at us strangely. Some of their eyes met mine but they quickly turned away. Dr. J ended their confusion. "Doctors, this is the boy about whom we have been reading." He smiled and took his hand from Stephen's head where it had rested, and gently placed it on my shoulder as a proud father would to his daughter.

"Today, Stephen is having a central line placed. Then he is going home with his mother. Four weeks ago I received a call from my associates at the Mayo Clinic. They asked me to assist them in evaluating lab work for a child that had no measurable fibrinogen in his blood and had not experienced a major bleed into any internal organ. I decided to come to Saint Paul and see for myself. I knew they must have made a mistake somewhere and I was determined to find it.

"When I arrived at the hospital it was late, but my curiosity would not wait until morning. I looked at Stephen's chart, spoke with the attending physician and still couldn't figure out where they had made the error. Before I went to examine the patient I went to Radiology to look at his x-rays. The radiologist was most helpful. We discussed this highly unusual case. In closing he had said to me, 'sometimes God uses the small ones to teach the wise.'

"I went to examine Stephen. I was greeted by his mother. Indian flute music was playing in the background. I had dozens of questions that I wanted to ask but when I got into the room I couldn't think of any. I drew some blood from Stephen myself and waited for the results. I sat down next to Stephen and his mom and studied the lab values. I hadn't found the clue to unravel this riddle, but I hoped to solve the mystery. Before I left in the morning, I asked his mother if she knew why Stephen was still alive.

"She said, 'Stephen has a purpose in life and he is going to be here until that purpose is served. Maybe God is using his small body to teach the experts.'

"The next few weeks I searched for a reasonable explanation. Many times I sat by his bed and held his hand. I knew I was holding the hand of a miracle. I tried to find the doctor of radiology that I previously talked with, but no one knew who he was. Apparently they don't staff a full-time night radiologist. Any questions?"

The group of doctors nervously shifted their weight from one side to the other. One of them said, "Excuse me, doctor. I don't understand."

Dr. J recapped. "This is Stephen. It was his lab values that we reviewed. The correct medical conclusion is that he has died. The correct medical conclusion is that one too many medical compromises against him existed for his body to handle. Medically speaking, there is no viable reason why he should have life. That's true. All of it is true."

He stood, paused, looked tenderly at Stephen and then into the residents' inquisitive eyes. "Some of you will use your career seeking answers to questions that you will not find," he said. "Others of you will pause long enough to be a part of life's miracles. Whatever you choose, remember it is not up to us as doctors who will live or who will die. It is up to us as doctors to utilize the tools that we have been given, use them to the best of our ability, learn, and go on. We do not give life and we cannot take life. That decision is not up to us as doctors."

Silence overtook the room. Some of the residents had tears in their eyes; others appeared uncomfortable and fidgety.

"Come, greet Stephen and his mom as we continue rounds." One by one the residents quietly followed him out of the Surgical Waiting Room. Dr. J patted me on the back, smiling broadly as he left the room. The residents filed out like a game of follow-the-leader. Some of them embraced me; some of them walked past without eye contact. Some gave Stephen a high-five; some touched his face, felt the softness of his skin. All passed by the Eagle Doctor. All were touched by his life.

Jesus Walked By

We fussed and we brushed until squeaky and clean
We were ready to get out in the public again
The wheelchair was polished all shiny and bright
And we tucked all the stuff in a place out of sight
Excited and happy to be out once again
We grinned and we laughed at the sounds all around
Mothers were shushing their little one's voices
As I longed to hear just one tiny whisper
We pushed down the street and into the diner
Where families sat eating and drinking for dinner
I opened the valve and held up the feeding
We felt very different even the way we were eating
Then out in the street the kids were all playing
Baseball and Frisbee and running and jumping
We watched from the corner and felt far away
Not a part of this world seemed to fit anymore
Then into one final little store we continued
To see what we'd missed as a part of this world
The storekeeper stopped by the wheelchair that day
He said not a word, not a sound, not an utter
Then all of a sudden he ran to the back
Had we offended him thoroughly with the sight of the chair
Or was he offended by the bags, tubes and the wires
We left that fine day, sought the refuge of home
Where we understood that our life's not our own
It is borrowed from heaven, it is only a loan
And the things that will stay are the things not our own
We had everything we needed right there in our home
The storekeeper called, had some news that he shared
When the chair wheeled by, he saw Jesus walk by
My boy remained strapped in the chair with a belt
His handicaps had purchased that place in the world
We thought that the shining and polishing would help
Be accepted by all, be all that they are
Instead we were reminded by the storekeeper that day
That Jesus walks by when we get out of the way.

CLN

Shaddy

Shadrack Josiah had been my best friend for sixteen years. He was the smartest dog and friendliest comrade I have ever encountered. His endless energy and playful character brought much-needed joy and balance to my sometimes serious quests.

When Stephen first came home with me from the hospital Shadrack would lie on the floor by his feet. Soon he was known as the "English General." He spent many hours with Stephen, quietly learning his every move, anticipating every breath. Not much time passed before Shadrack was able to recognize Stephen's many medical compromises before they occurred.

I became busy with the ancillary support needs and endless training of caregivers. Shadrack, on the other hand, simply spent time with Stephen. Normally when I would sleep at night Shaddy would sleep at the foot of my bed. Sometimes he would wander into Stephen's room and move things until he could lie under Stephen's bed. The nurses tried to lure him out with treats and bones, but he wouldn't move. Soon Stephen would have a seizure and the room would become a whirlwind of stabilizing activity.

Repeated visits by Shadrack to Stephen's bedside soon prompted Stephen's caregivers to get the intervening medicine ready. Over and over again, Shadrack would communicate Stephen's needs without words.

One day I was busy preparing the evening meal. Stephen was resting comfortably in his room listening to the music of Raffi. Shadrack paced around the kitchen floor under my feet.

Soon he tugged at my pants leg and won my attention. He led me to Stephen's room.

Stephen was grooving to the music. He was smiling and content. Shadrack found his way under Stephen's bed, while I turned to walk out of Stephen's room. Two steps later I was stopped by the blast of one of Stephen's alarms. Stephen was having a major seizure.

Hours later, I sat crumpled in the chair next to Stephen's bed. His portacath had been accessed, intravenous seizure-stopping medicine given, while I breathed for him with the ambu bag. The room was littered with the remnants of this latest crisis. Wrappers that protected sterile gloves, needles, bandages, and vials of medications littered the room. Stephen was stable. Shadrack scooted out from under Stephen's bed. The angel dog nuzzled up to me and rested.

I stroked his soft fur and thanked God that he had been found. Years before, Shadrack had somehow wandered away from the house where I was staying in Mississippi. It was a hot July day and he did not greet me when I returned home. I looked everywhere for him. Hours turned into days.

Missing posters were hung around town and the surrounding forest and swampland were searched. On the back roads in the "wayward" country, I stopped at a little shanty to inquire about my lost dog. A big man sat in a rocking chair. In his hand he held a shotgun and as I approached he pointed the gun in my direction. Someone had told me minutes before that a dog fitting my description had been seen walking toward this man's house. But I was instructed to "stay away from the man—he hasn't come off that porch in years."

I had to know if he had seen my dog. Shadrack might be

hurt and need me. He might be hungry or thirsty. The incredible agony of not knowing what had happened to someone I loved was stronger than my fear of looking down the barrel of that shotgun.

When I got about twenty feet from the man, he yelled, "Stop!" I stopped. With the gun still pointed at me, he said, "Speak your piece. I can kill you now. You're on my land."

I literally fell to the ground sobbing, and screamed, "I lost my dog! I lost my dog! He may be hurt. I have to find him." I lay on the ground totally overcome by grief, its powerful force pressing me to the hot earth. Time had no power, no authority.

My heaves of sorrow were interrupted by a hand, pressing on my shoulder. I looked up to see the old man looking down at me. He knelt beside me on one knee, his tattered overalls hanging around his thin body. He looked at me as if he'd seen a ghost. With one hand he steadied himself. With the other he held a glass of water. His shotgun stood propped in the corner on the porch. He placed the water carefully down on ground and reached for me with his hand.

He spoke quietly. "Grief so great is not experienced by this Earth's inhabitants. I will help you, angel girl."

The old man helped me off the ground. We sat on the porch and talked. Thirteen years earlier he had lost his dog—a liver-and-white English springer spaniel, just like my Shadrack Josiah. He had stayed in his little shanty waiting for him to return. He didn't go to the store or even walk to his mailbox. He didn't sleep in his bed or bathe in his house; if he did, he might miss his dog's return. "He may have lost his way," he said.

He lit a lantern and we made some grits and toast. Sly had been a preacher before his dog left and the church people still dropped food off to him. "They throw it in the yard," he said, smiling. "I became bitter. God took my friend. He took my only friend." The company of understood sorrow erected a break-water that eased the waves of our grief.

I said goodbye to my new-found friend and left without having found my dog. Somehow, in that exchange, I decided and pledged to God that no matter what happened, I would not curse Him. I had not and would not choose to use this time to turn on my Master. I was determined to continue, somehow.

I went home and started to catch up on some of the work I had let go the four days Shadrack had been missing. The phone rang. "Get over here quick. We may have found your dog." I hung up the phone and ran toward the door before I realized that I had no idea who had just called. Frantic, I grabbed my jacket and keys and headed toward the car. Lights were coming up the driveway. I ran toward them, yelling, "Move! Move! I have to go!"

Driving the van was a nice-looking middle-aged man wearing a suit; behind him was a lady. In the passenger seat sat my new friend Sly. He was smiling. He said, "Come on, hurry. I think we found your dog." I climbed into the First Baptist Church van. We rode to where the dog was seen but he wasn't there anymore.

I thanked the couple and we drove to Sly's home to drop him off. When we arrived at his house, there on the porch sitting next to the rocking chair, was a dog that looked just like my Shaddy. Sly got out of the van and walked to his porch. The dog stood up and wagged his tail. He greeted Sly. Sly and Shadrack jumped up and down, and played like two long-lost friends. Sly laid on the ground where I had earlier that day. This time I knelt down beside him and offered my hand to help him up. The couple that had been in the van watched this scene with surprise and the kind of awe that occurs during a human birth.

Soon the four of us sat in Sly's kitchen. Shadrack lay at Sly's feet. The man and woman were Sly's sister and brother-in-law. Thirteen years earlier they had left Sly on that porch, having given up on him and his vigil. They had come by only to throw groceries into the yard.

Shadrack and I went home. Sly went home with his sister and family to live. Today he is preaching again.

All of us were formed from the ground
And we are all buried in the earth

While alive we are buried by our limits
Our love has boundaries
Our deeds have limits
Our energy ends

When our bodies return to the ground
And return to their original form
Then, and only then are we free
Free to live with our Creator
Limitless light
Unending love

CLN

Ambulance Seizure

The night's darkness was interrupted by the flash of lights as the ambulance approached our home, its shrill siren piercing the stillness. The sleepy world I had just been enjoying was instantly transformed into the harsh reality of epilepsy.

This wasn't the first time that life's movement stopped as a seizure began. Moments before, Stephen's caregiver had aroused me with an anxious voice, "Stephen is having a seizure and he is not breathing."

The rest my body craved would have to wait. As my physical self struggled to wake up, my mind took control and I began dictating familiar orders. Entering Stephen's room, I grabbed the ambu and began breathing for him. The plastic bag that I rhythmically squeezed was now supplying oxygen to his distorted body. He glanced up at me with his eyes and a slight lopsided smile crossed his face.

I yearned to find words of comfort to soothe his soul as his body cried for relief. Gently caressing his head and kissing his cheek, I acknowledged the disgust and anger I owned for epilepsy. This disease was part of my son.

Love would bridge the gap between my sweet boy and this horrific disease. Love would allow me to be the breath of life that my son needed. Love would be stronger then the overwhelming responsibility that I now faced.

The paramedics arrived. One of them asked, "What can I do?" Before I could speak, the captain did. "You get the stretcher ready. You get his history. You get the hospital on the radio."

Like a well-tuned machine, these men accomplished their directives. The captain now stood alongside me and touched Stephen's head gently. "I am here to help you and your mom," he said. "We will get you feeling better."

The confidence in his voice soothed my aching heart. Medications were given, vital signs taken, and still Stephen's body was captured by this event. The hospital doctor requested that Stephen be transferred to the Emergency Room for stabilization.

Continuing to breathe for Stephen, I watched as muscle contortions captured his face. I wiped beads of sweat from his face as we entered the ambulance. The stillness of the night caressed the earth, but somehow we were not a part of it anymore. Inside the ambulance I was allowed to continue breathing for Stephen. His seizure continued with increasing difficulty as his airways became more constricted. His color was poor, and concern gripped the paramedics' faces. The captain continued to choreograph this dance; we waltzed robotically to his voice.

Swaying with the movement of increased speed, the captain observed Stephen: "He needs more oxygen or he's not going to make it." Our waltz slowed.

One of the paramedics radioed the Emergency Room doctor: "We're in trouble here. We're about twelve minutes out. We've given all the medications you ordered. We have been unable to start an IV. His vital signs are getting worse and—" his voice was interrupted by a nurse on the radio. "Just a minute, ah, hold two seconds, okay?"

Seconds seemed like hours as I glanced at the paramedics' faces. Minutes ago we were strangers. Now here we were, detached from our histories, personal lives, homes, and families. We were detached together, sharing my son's pain. I marveled at God weaving our lives together.

A familiar voice transmitted over the radio. "Is his mother with him?" The captain answered, "Yes."

"Chris, Stephen's not going to make it to the hospital if he doesn't get some oxygen into those lungs. You have two choices. You need to force air into his lungs, which may result in his airway tearing as it has before. Or, he will die. It's up to you."

Silence, piercing silence. The words danced wildly as I stared at the city lights through the speeding ambulance window. Our slow dance was replaced by some fast-paced clumsy ritual. How could the night convey so much peace to its inhabitants and to us such catastrophe?

My despair was interrupted by the captain's hand on my shoulder, firmly but gently demanding my attention. He looked straight into my eyes. The decision I would make was unconditionally accepted by this stranger, Stephen's rescuer and now my friend. He wiped the tears that had fallen from my eyes onto Stephen's face. With the same strong hand that had given me strength he comforted my son.

I leaned over and kissed my sweet son's face and while humming, "Jesus loves me, this I know . . .," I forced air into his lungs. I held my breath. All eyes focused on Stephen. We waited. A modest relaxation was felt in Stephen's chest when I delivered the next breath. The paramedics sighed with relief. The waltz began again as we continued to the hospital. One of the medics radioed the hospital ER, "It's a go. We'll see you in a few minutes."

And He saith unto me,
"My grace is sufficient for you,
for My strength is made
perfect in weakness."

2 Corinthians 12:9

In the Almighty's Arms

Stephen's stretcher was ushered through the open doors of the Saint Paul Children's Hospital Emergency Room, escorted by nurses and doctors. The lights overhead were bright, artificially shattering night's darkness. Sounds of monitors, alarms and other man-made machines assisted God's masterfully created shells that occupied the rooms. Each person fought to preserve life in the comfortable shell that surrounded him, while his soul yearned to go home. The battle of life and death escalated. Either way, Stephen would win.

Stephen entered Trauma 1—a large room filled with medicine's most advanced intervention supplies and equipment. His fragile body continued to seize. Two doctors and two nurses tried to penetrate his veins through his skin. They hoped to achieve a direct way into his body through the body's pipeline. That way, seizure-stopping medicine could be given.

Stephen lay on the cot in the middle of the bright room, his eyes closed. The respiratory therapist had taken over breathing for him with the ambu bag. His stethoscope laid on Stephen's chest, monitoring each breath. He was careful to "do no harm."

Multiple sticks were made and I asked them to stop drilling holes into my son for awhile. Instead of a nurturing, loving mother I felt like an accomplice in a rape. Trying to soothe my son's heaving body, I stroked his cheeks and brushed the hair from his eyes. I shielded his eyes against the bright lights with my other hand. Whispering to him that I loved him, I wondered how much pain his little body could handle. I struggled with suffering's mask.

"Chris, I'm sorry, we have to get a line in. We have to keep trying." They agreed to only stick through his skin one at a time. The others continued to wrap tourniquets around his extremities in pursuit of a vein. I longed to hold him in my arms and protect him from the pain he was experiencing. Stephen's body had been seizing for over an hour and every cell shouted with pain. Continuing to kneel down at his side and careful not to hinder the dance around me, I studied Stephen's peaceful face. Not a wrinkled brow, not a frown were evident. His face did not reflect the painful chaos inside him. When asked to respond, he blinked his eyes or squeezed an offered hand. Just a tiny move, but he did respond.

The room seemed to disappear, like the skyline of a city fades away into fog. The outline was visible, the city existed as it had—it just faded away. The light refracted in the fog and its particles absorbed the sound around it. The room was quiet now, light but not blinding or abrasive. A familiar peace was felt all around. As the fog enveloped me it penetrated each cell of my body.

"What's this?" Slowly, I saw an Emergency Room below me. Hustling and bustling doctors and nurses worked feverishly around a small shell that laid in the middle of the room. A form knelt at the boy's left side. Concern covered her face. Monitors beeped, alarms blared, lights blinded. But in the light suspended over this room, it was quiet. It was soothing; it was peaceful. There in the corner of the room, I held my Stephen and he was at peace. He did not feel the sticks, the pokes, the procedures that were being performed below us.

A tunnel filled with light was beside us to our left. It was a large round tunnel filled with foggy light particles. Its edges were dense light forms. They had shape by light. A bright glow beckoned us at the end of the tunnel. Gently, movement was felt all around us. In this aura, my Stephen could run, jump, breathe, lick an ice cream cone, sing. His soul was limitless. Still, he remained in my arms. I held his soul.

"Chris, Chris, we got the line in and the medication is running. It looks like he is going to make it after all!"

"Okay, doctor, thanks . . . I think."

Stephen opened his eyes and looked up at the corner of the room. He looked at me and smiled. I had experienced a holy place. Children's bodies do not feel hurt when they are in the arms of the Almighty. The able arms are always present. Stephen knew this; now I did too. I helped the nurses bandage the eleven new sticks in his skin. I gently kissed each band-aid.

The seizure stopped. I dressed him, scooped him into my arms, maneuvered the medical equipment around us, and hailed a taxi. We were going home.

The breezes at dawn have secrets to tell
Don't go back to sleep
Ask for what you really want
Don't go back to sleep
People are moving back and forth
Across the threshold where
The two worlds touch
The door is round and open
Don't go back to sleep.

Mirabi (Ninth Century)

Nightwatch

We were home again from another ICU visit, but this time with IV antibiotics and many new medical machines. Later, one of his regular nurses was coming to care for him and I could look forward to a healing night of sleep. Since Stephen had been in the ICU, sleep had become rare. When his condition was critical, I had stayed at his bedside. When the doctor walked in his hospital room and said, "Chris, I think he's going to pull through," I had collapsed. I had used up all my energy, and now I was to care for him at home. I didn't know where I would find the strength.

In the morning, I poured a quick cup of strong coffee and proceeded to Stephen's bedroom. "I can do this," I repeated on the way down the hall. "No problem!" The night nurse had gone, leaving me in charge of Stephen's care until evening.

This was the first morning Stephen had slept in his own bed since the addition of the c-pap machine. It had helped him breathe easier through his collapsing airways. Hopefully his remaining strength would be saved, creating energy to enjoy life a little more. Since—miraculously—he had grown, his body weight had resulted in increased airway constriction due to the heaviness on his lungs. I shook my head in disbelief as I looked at him peacefully resting. He had gained weight—a blessing. Now that double-edged sword cut from the other side. It was too much weight for his fragile airways.

Regaining my composure, I made sure all the necessary tubes and wires were ready to change from this breathing circuit to oxygen through his trach mask without the machine.

When he began to waken, he wanted the machine off. Leaving it on to breathe with him made him anxious. As his anxiety increased, he became frightened; then the new machine designed to help him breathe became a hollow vacuum.

I shrugged, reminding myself that I could handle this. My pep talk continued. Tubes in position, medications given, I was ready to help Stephen make his transition from sleep to comfortable awareness.

Waiting for him to waken, I called Saint Paul Children's Hospital to update Dr. M, as requested. I was excited to tell him that we were doing just fine with the new mechanical addition to our family.

It was about 10 a.m. Usually Dr. M was busy in clinic at that time, so I would leave a message and he could return my call later. "Hang on, Chris," the clinic secretary said, "I'll get Dr. M. He's been waiting for you to call."

"Okay, I'll wait," I said. Not more than two seconds passed and Stephen started moving. I propped the phone under my chin and started the process of changing over the breathing circuit so Stephen could get his needed oxygen without the machine creating the vacuum effect that alarmed him.

I accidentally pulled the phone out of the wall, disconnecting the call. Running back to the kitchen, I grabbed the cordless phone and propped it under my chin. The same song was playing. Good, I hadn't missed Dr. M—he would know that I can handle this!

Wiping my brow, I sang a good-morning song to Stephen and continued futzing with the tubing. His oxcimeter alarm went off. *Be-duboop-dodo.* Stephen was doing just fine. The alarm beeped continuously because his toe was wriggling.

I leaned over him to unhook his new c-pap machine and the phone dropped from under my chin onto his pillow. Oops. I started laughing. Where was the organization that had been here just a minute ago? My eyes were tearing from laughing so hard that I could hardly see which piece of tubing to connect with another. Stephen started laughing, too, which set the apnea monitor off into its noisy ritual of *BLEEP BLEEP.*

"Hello, hello." Oh, where was that phone? I couldn't find the phone. The doorbell rang. They would go away or come back later, I hoped. It rang again.

"Hey, anyone in there?" I could hardly hear the voice but knew someone was there because the dogs were in the back-yard barking loudly.

"Hello," I heard from the phone. "Hello," I heard from the front door. Tubing in hand, now not certain what to do with which parts, laughing, I just hollered "Come in" to whoever was at the front door. I found the phone that had fallen, caus-ing a *boomp* noise when it hit Stephen's drum under the bed. This brought on more uncontrollable laughter from Stephen.

"Dr. M? Hi. We're okay. Hold on a minute," as I again dropped the phone. The lady who had been at the door was now standing in front of me.

"Honey," she said, "you've got to go out and get your dog. One of the dogs has got his head stuck in the fence and I'm afraid he's going to hang himself."

Oh boy. I had this tubing straightened out before. "Chris, Chris, is everything okay over there?" was heard coming from the phone. Standing at Stephen's bedside, I looked down at

Stephen and say "Pray buddy, pray." He laughed.

I needed to talk with Dr. M, get the tubing straightened out and get our dog unstuck. Our laughter continued as the lady whom I had never seen before ran outside to see if she could get the dog out of the fence.

I finally found the correct pieces of tubing and connected Stephen to his oxygen. The doorbell rang again—ah, a familiar voice. My friend from across the street ran into the hall toward Stephen's room. We collided in the doorway as I turned to run and meet her. Picking each other up from the floor, she told me she, too, had come to help my dog. As she headed toward the back door, I told her of the lady who had just gone out to do the same thing.

Quiet. A second of quiet. The alarms silenced, the dogs quit barking, our laughter subsided. Then, again the doorbell rang.

This time it was the police. "I got a call from Children's Hospital. They said you might need some help. The medics are on their way."

Oh no, the phone! I had forgotten the phone!

Asking him to come in, I returned to Stephen's room and reassured the officer that we were fine. The paramedics arrived. I found the phone under Stephen's bed. "Dr. M?"

"Just a minute, Chris," a nurse answered. "Is everything okay over there? How's Stephen?"

~~~

Despite some frantic moments, home care is usually pleasant. It provides a way for ill or disabled children and adults to live in their own homes. Without adequate support, many people would have to exist within the walls of institutions. Sometimes, however, that is the best decision that can be made.

Stephen and I were thankful for programs that allowed him to grow at home. Even with support, the job of home care is difficult. The family and other caregivers fill many roles: head nurse, secretary, physical therapist, occupational therapist, speech therapist, respiratory therapist, equipment manager, teacher, translator, housekeeper, cook, in-service director, playmate, liaison, and counselor.

Often managing all these responsibilities is exhausting. The family's role does not stop at 5 p.m. There is no Happy Hour at six o'clock. The care they provide continues twenty-four hours a day, seven days a week. Often they train and assist the nurses and therapists.

The primary caregivers are always on call, no matter where they are or what time it is. They are responsible for providing for their loved ones. The final decision surrounding all aspects of care resides with them. They carry out the wishes of their loved ones.

The workload is somewhat similar to having a sick infant all of the time. The interruption of life's normal routine becomes the norm. Privacy is invaded. Private space is diminished with every different caregiver who enters the home. A different vocabulary is developed. Dishes are used, food eaten and conversations listened to—much the way a celebrity's life is invaded, but without the paycheck.

Stress becomes a constant companion as routines are dismissed and personal time is diminished. Serenity is aided by those who take over the hands-on care for a time. Respite becomes a tool of survival.

When someone chooses to shine a light in a seemingly dark world, help comes from limitless sources and diverse ways.

Families are one source. Caregivers are another. Stephen has had many different caregivers in his lifetime. Each one of them has been a gift. Regardless of their differences as human beings, they have chosen to ease the lives of the people in their care. Most of the time they care unconditionally. Nurses work long hours with little compensation. Therapists, teachers, vendors, pharmacists, hospice workers, social workers, chaplains often exhaust themselves to supply assistance beyond what their paychecks reflect.

Our society hosts many award ceremonies, yet those who provide care to the silent ones remain thankless. Their deeds and acts of kindness arise from their spirits and meet the heavens, where they will be rewarded in time.

Friends plant flowers along the pathway of the silent ones. Some plant roses of listening, others plant tulips of kind acts. Some bring food, others work the ground and water growing friendship. Doctors provide direct care. They pave the way for stabilization, providing day-to-day assistance for the bodies of the silent ones and their caregivers. They wrestle with political cutbacks and policy changes.

Sometimes, though, differences in caregivers' views on life collide.

~~~

Stephen was snug in his bed one evening. All of the new medical equipment and IV solutions had found a home. The paperwork was in order and rest could begin. After giving a thorough and lengthy report to the on-coming nurse, I fell into my own bed. It swallowed me up quickly with its familiarity.

I was only asleep for a short time when I awoke suddenly and bolted to Stephen's room without really knowing why. I was halfway there before I realized I was walking. Turning the corner to Stephen's room, I found the nurse—my trusted relief— with a syringe in her hand.

That wasn't too unusual as Stephen's IV often required flushing. The look on her face, however, was foreign. Sweat was dripping from her forehead. She looked at me standing in the doorway and said, "I'm going to help you. I'm going to end his pain."

I walked closer to her and she screamed, "Stop. Don't come any closer."

I was confused. I told her that Stephen didn't look like he needed any pain medication. He was asleep. His vital signs were stable. I told her that the oral pain medication was working and that he didn't need much of it anymore.

"You don't get it, do you?" she said. "I am going to ease his pain forever. You will finally get the help that you need."

I stood facing her by Stephen's bed. I struggled to comprehend what she was saying. She walked toward me and began to push me backwards. The mysterious invisible boundary had been crossed. I asked her to hand me the syringe and she just swung it in my face. I prayed that I was having a nightmare.

I called on the powerful warrior angels that inhabited our home and she dropped the syringe. Its contents spilled onto the carpet. She looked at Stephen and looked at me as if waking from hibernation.

"Oh my God," she cried, "I almost killed your baby!" and ran out of the house.

I cared for Stephen that night.

Buffalo Tatanka

The buffalo was sustenance and life to the Sioux. It was also shelter and warmth. Buffalo is provisions, shelter, and thanksgiving. The Sioux regard buffalo also as abundance.

from the book
Mother Earth Spirituality
by Ed McGaa, Eagle Man

Buffalo's Way

I stood frozen, gripping the receiver of the phone until the dial tone interrupted my shock. Sliding to the floor, using the wall as my guide, I crumbled. The intact system that had been created to protect the rights of children, formatted to provide services that allow families to nurture special-needs children at home, now hindered me. Using the programs in place to their fullest extent, I struggled to maintain equilibrium and a sense of normalcy. The system that had allowed me to bring Stephen from the hospital to my home wanted to snatch him back.

The words reverberated: "We didn't think that he would live this long." How could one person's message interrupt my life so callously? How could the same person who conveyed congratulations when we first arrived home now relay this opposite message so calmly? How can programs just stop?

What about my son? How could he understand? He was thriving outside hospital walls, not merely existing. What form would love take for my son now? We would find a way to continue together. There had to be another program that would provide for Stephen. I would not let them take him back. I would not let them take him without a fight.

Sobbing, I held Stephen close to me. My heart knew that to put him back in the hospital now, and leave him there until another program was found, would hurt him. I looked at him and saw an innocent child. He was content—at last.

As a lioness protects her cub, rage began to build within me. Righteous indignation intensified as we prayed. Suddenly, we were transferred to another time, another place—Stephen's time. I covered him with my body, bending over him and sheltering his body with my own. He wore my skin for his armor. Arrows flew; their shrill sounds permeated the air all around us. They were the arrows of indifference, budget cuts, balanced bottom-lines, incompetence.

The arrows touched me. Some grazed my skin, some pierced it. Lingering in this danger zone, we were aware of the magnitude of this war. We represented the families that have children with disabilities needing financial and governmental help. We reflected their fortitude. Their energy sustained us.

One of the arrows cut through my chest and hit Stephen. He winced and I realized that he was hurt. His life was impeded by these system promises that had not materialized and/or were changing to save money. Painfully, I cried as another arrow fully cut my leg, lodging in Stephen.

He would die. Without financial consideration and the programs' continuation, he would not remain home. He would return to the hospital and he would die there. The voice of the system person—I thought, of my friend—continued to echo, "I'm sorry, there is nothing I can do. The money set aside for special-needs children is being reassigned to assist universal health care. We have determined that most of the children in our program are not productive to society. They spend our money and then they die."

Powerfully and unexpectedly Stephen and my tears were dried by a cloud of dust. A roar was heard from a distance. The ground shook as we sat on the quaking earth. My eyes were gritty with the dirt that swirled around us. My tongue explored the fine sand in my mouth. As the cloud darkened, the arrows began to miss their intended mark. The exhaustion, the bleeding, the sobs, became faint as the sound of the stampede approached. I held Stephen as the gathering of this arrow-interrupter came closer.

When the dust settled, we were surrounded by buffalo. They had produced a circle around us that protected us from enemy arrows. One of them lay close to us toward our left. The others stood side by side facing us, creating a hedge—impenetrable by earthly arrows. We were safe. I bound my son's wounds and we recovered in the presence of these protectors. This battle had been won. The war continued.

The sun's sparkles shone through my parents' picture window as I rose from the floor, still cradling Stephen in my arms. I struggled to reacclimatize myself to this Earth. My ears rang and my whole body was drenched in an Almighty presence.

"Chrissy, what's wrong? You will never believe what happened to me just a minute ago. Are you okay?" My mom was kindly waiting for me to regain my composure. She continued, "I was on my way to the mailbox and out of nowhere a dust storm came up. I couldn't see to keep going so I just stopped in the driveway and prayed. I heard a loud noise that started far away and it kept coming closer. The ground shook where I knelt and I saw you holding Stephen in your arms and you were bleeding. Are you sure you're okay?"

After I reassured her that I was all right, she went on. "I'm not sure what kind of animals got loose, but they sure were noisy! There were a lot of them, too. I didn't see them, but they sounded like herds of big horses. Your father just got home and said it smelled like buffalo. Are you sure you're okay?"

Some think our life is different
A life that they cannot cross
They think that only we feel loss
That stress is something else
They isolate us from themselves
Like lepers pleading space
When all along this world we walk
Side by side yet far apart
If for a moment we would stop
And look right at each other
We would find life's mysteries solved
For we are one with each other

CLN

Mrs. Rooney's Fifth-grade Class

"All right, class, come to order. Take your seats, everyone. We have a lot of work to do before lunch." Mrs. Rooney's fifth-grade class quickly erected an organized expanse from chairs, desks, backpacks and notebooks. Her soft voice was heard above the quieting chatter.

"Class, it's time to form groups for the science fair!" Excited eyes darted back and forth with nods of agreement when friends met one another's eyes. Seated at their desks, they eagerly awaited their teacher's next directive. Not a voice or a rustle was heard as she assumed her place in front of the twenty-seven eager fifth-graders. The only sound that was heard was a constant *Ssssssshhhhhhh* of oxygen as its flow offered Stephen much needed assistance. He sat attentive, too, awaiting further instructions.

"Okay class, now we will choose teams for this year's science fair. The winner will be treated to a spring event yet to be decided. It will involve a few days away from school!" There was a roar of applause as she placed each student's name in a goldfish bowl.

Four excited students took their places in the front of the class. They had earned the prestigious title of science fair engineers by their peers following the previous week's study of artifacts. Lucy stretched her hand into the fishbowl first. Her curly red hair bounced as she squealed with delight, announcing one of her good friend's names.

Wally slowly and stiffly reached his hand into the bowl,

removing a piece of paper that revealed another name. Forcing his hand into the bowl and mixing the papers, Eddy shuffled and shuffled the papers until the class burst out in laughter. Mrs. Rooney quickly regained control with a darting glance above the small glasses perched on the tip of her nose. Eddy finally chose a name. Last, Brittany put her small hand into the bowl, and timidly smiled as she read aloud the name of a student who would be a part of her team. She hoped Stephen would be on her team—they were friends.

When all the names had been drawn, the students were instructed to form a circle around their prospective leaders. Mrs. Rooney's final instructions were for the team including Stephen to gather around his wheelchair. That was easier than maneuvering his chair around the crowded room.

Eddy stood next to Stephen. "Mrs. Rooney, Mrs. Rooney," he called, as his hand flapped trying desperately to gain her attention.

"Yes, Eddy, how can I help you?" said Mrs. Rooney.

"I don't think Stephen should be a part of this," Eddy replied. "Can't you give him something else to do like you usually do?" Standing tall and proud, he awaited her response.

Mrs. Rooney said flatly, "Team number three, Stephen is a part of your team as well as he is a part of this class."

Eddy shuffled nervously, hardly believing what his teacher had said. Conferring with some of the other astounded students in his group, he continued much more loudly. She must not have heard him correctly. Clearing his throat, he blurted out, "Stephen can't do anything. It's not fair!"

"Class dismissed for lunch. See you in forty minutes," was Mrs. Rooney's response.

Disgusted, yet happily receiving pats of comfort on the back from his teammates, he strutted out to lunch. The room was quiet, except for the *Sssssssshhhh* of Stephen's oxygen.

His nurse wiped a tear from Stephen's eye, smiled at him and said, "It'll be okay, Stephen. They don't understand. Wait and see. It'll work out all right." She quietly continued to perform the many medical interventions Stephen needed before the students resumed their positions in the classroom.

This lunchtime had been tougher than most. Usually music and laughter had filled the room, but not today. Neither one of them felt much like music. The misunderstanding of Stephen's physical disabilities had undeniably created a silent chasm that exaggerated differences. The rest of the school day ended uneventfully for the students in Mrs. Rooney's class. Stephen's school day ended, too.

Mrs. Rooney's class convened the next day without Stephen in attendance. Illness often prevented him from being a visible part of the active classroom. Michael, Stephen's friend and neighbor, volunteered to bring Stephen classroom material and homework.

At 3:45 the doorbell rang at our house. "Hi, Stephen, how are you? I brought you some school stuff." Stephen's spirit radiated in Michael's enthusiasm as he told Stephen all about his day. Stephen's nurse sat in the corner of the room wondering why this nice boy couldn't be on Stephen's science fair team. This year, most of the other fifth-graders who ridiculed him or ignored him comprised the team. The thought of meeting them again at school tomorrow was unsettling. She was relieved by the sight of two best friends exchanging laughter. Stephen and Michael had crossed the bridge of difference. They played and spent time together, enjoying common interests. Stephen's disabilities and Michael's heritage existed only on the surface of their friendship. It had no further depth and caused no inconvenience. It simply existed.

The following week, Mrs. Rooney's fifth-grade class met in groups to further brainstorm about their science fair projects. At the students' request, the groups met in separate rooms. Rumor had it that many a science fair championship had been lost due to the pirating of opposing teams' ideas.

Eddy's team met in the classroom. This year's science fair project was dedicated to "man's advances in electricity." Ideas were feverishly being explored.

BEEP. One of the alarms on Stephen's machines blared, interrupting Rachel's verbal contribution. "Whoops, I forgot," she said, scowling at Stephen. *Bbbiiiizzzzzz* interrupted another student's attempt to contribute his opinion to the group. Soon, without much accomplished, the brainstorming session was over.

"Class, time to come together. Will the leaders please come to the front of the room." Further instructions were given by Mrs. Rooney that each leader would report on the progress of the team without revealing their individual selection.

It was Eddy's turn. Normally Eddy was the dude, the in-control leader of the classroom. When Eddy spoke, everyone was attentive. Today he wished the classroom floor would swallow him up. How could he face his fellow classmates? How could he reveal that his group was not making the same progress that the other groups were?

He took his place in front of the classroom and sheepishly began. "We have not agreed on the direction of our project."

Tenaciously he continued, "As a matter of fact, we can't even think. Stephen keeps interrupting us. Mrs. Rooney, please can we pick names again?"

Beeeepppp. It was one of Stephen's machine alarms—another tear rolled silently down his cheek.

"See what I mean!" Eddy said excitedly, pointing at Stephen. "All those things make too much noise!"

Other than the constant *Sssssssshhh* of oxygen, the room was quiet. Very quiet. A few students cringed at Eddy"s boldness, others smirked with pleasure. Eddy would say the things out loud that some only silently thought.

Mrs. Rooney rose sternly from her desk in the back corner of the room. She walked purposefully toward the front of the classroom. Even without hearing a word, the students knew they were in trouble. Cultural differences, color, economic positions, and variable physical attributes did not exist at this moment. They all knew she was upset.

Before Mrs. Rooney reached her place in front of the students, Eddy suddenly said, "Stop, wait a minute! Our team is okay. Stephen stays. He's in."

Most of the students thought Eddy was desperately trying to thwart Mrs. Rooney's wrath. Eddy, however, took his seat just as piously and as proudly as if he had won a blue ribbon at the county fair. Before he sat down, he walked over to Stephen and gave him a low-five. The class was abuzz with whisper and wonderment. No one would know for another seven weeks what had transpired that day. Eddy and Stephen knew and so did Mrs. Rooney.

~~~

It was the day before Halloween and class adjourned for the

day. The next day, the fall party would be held. Excitement filled the halls of the school. Before the party began each science fair team would make some final adjustments to their projects. Eddy's team had been a whirlwind of activity.

And then, the party began. Mrs. Rooney's class hunted for leaves, branches, nuts and whatever else they could find to make mobiles. They dined on trail mix as they marveled at their "nature creations."

Stephen missed the fifth-grade fall party, his life again interrupted by a compromising cold. Later that night, there would be Halloween trick-or-treating. Costumes and makeup would transform kids into Teenage Ninjas and romantic princesses. Soon the sun would go down and a fantastical array of active children would come out. They would run from house to house collecting edible treasures.

At our house, the day was progressing a bit differently. Even a slight cold could immobilize Stephen's body. His spirit wanted desperately to attend the fall party. His body craved more oxygen. At home he enjoyed his favorite music, but he would have rather been at school.

"Michael's here!" I called out, but Stephen was asleep. Difficult breathing had kept him awake most of the night.

"Is Stephen going to be all right?" asked Michael.

"Yes, Michael, I think he'll be okay. He has a cold," I explained.

~~~

Michael and I had become good friends. His family had moved in next door and the geographical space we shared was not flawed by the myth of handicaps.

Many people simply avoided contact with us. Some crossed

the street in front of us so as not to walk too close to us.

At Christmastime the previous year, Stephen was by my side at the school winter program. Doting parents groomed their children. Parents lined the gymnasium with video cameras, and grandmas and grandpas sat proudly with their young grandchildren in their laps.

The program had been about to commence. Stephen and I maneuvered into the crowded room and found a place to sit close to the front. To most of the parents in the school, we were the "new kids on the block." Frequent illness had prevented Stephen from attending class regularly. Unless our paths crossed in the neighborhood, most parents remained unknown. Today we were strangers.

One of the fathers merged an entire row of people into another row to vacate two open seats directly in front of the stage. This was no easy task, as the row consisted of twenty-three people with all their personal belongings.

Accepting this act of kindness, I moved Stephen up to the front. Smiling in acknowledgment, I thanked the man.

The first half of the program ended with hardy applause. Stretching during the intermission, the same man—the "row-mover"—approached me.

"Don't think for one minute that you're fooling anyone. I moved these people out of the way so you couldn't hurt them. We don't want your kind here," he declared.

My mind flashed back to a time when I was intimidated by the Ku Klux Klan in Mississippi, but this was an affluent Midwest suburb. Standing before me was not a man hiding behind a white robe and mask but a man with a suit and tie. He was clean-shaven and oozed prosperity. I could not believe what I was hearing.

"Excuse me?" I asked.

Even more loudly, he continued, "Why don't you just go home. You're jeopardizing the health of our community. You are putting us in danger."

I simply could not believe what I was hearing. He leaned over to pick up Stephen's medical bag from the floor and that was it. The ever-present, non-visible boundary line had been crossed. With all the patience I could retrieve to keep my composure, I reached for his hand. He dropped Stephen's medical bag and backed away from me as if we had re-entered the eighteenth century and I had leprosy! A part of me wanted, like Eddy, to sink into the floor, but another part wanted to hurt him back.

Covering Stephen's ears, I said to an unusually quiet room, "I don't understand. What is it that you want?"

He lunged toward me again. "You are not welcome here."

I replied through tears, "Stephen attends school here. This is a public building. We have as much right to be here as you."

This poised man sarcastically grinned and roared back, "You should have thought of that before you went ahead and slept around and got what you deserved!"

Finally, still covering Stephen's ears, I understood. This self-assured yet ignorant person was worried about HIV—at least I thought that was what he was alluding to. I released my hands from Stephen's ears and said, "You look like a very prosperous gentleman." He nodded in affirmation. "You also look like a very educated man." Again he nodded in agreement. "Then you know that the child you hold in your arms, sniffling and sneezing, proposes more health risks to those around us than does my son."

Looking about the room, I became aware that a large group of people had huddled behind this man. Behind Stephen and me stood an empty stage. People were straining to get closer to hear this interesting conversation. Some video cameras were still taping. I proceeded to give them a three-minute lecture on HIV—one normally reserved for young children. I wanted to make sure they had information they could assimilate.

My exhortation on HIV ended with, "Stephen is my foster son. His mother died, but not of AIDs. I will be happy to provide you our AIDs test results as soon as you show me yours."

The intermission ended and Stephen and I sat right where we were. The row-mover sat behind me—directly behind me. The winter program that year was long remembered by the "show during intermission." When I covered Stephen's ears in an attempt to shelter him from one man's ignorance, I immediately knew how to handle the horrible situation before me. I did not handle it. God handled it through me. Once again, He had to get me out of the away so He could work.

~~~

My path with the row-mover crossed again in spring the following year. Stephen and I were out for a walk. We enjoyed walking in the late evening as the sun was setting. The sidewalks were filled with children riding their bikes and adults walking. The ice-cream truck's bell echoed in the distance. We turned a corner to see a small group of people gathered in the middle of the street.

"Go get help! Call 911!" was heard from a familiar voice. The row-man was standing over a crying boy with an obviously misaligned leg. His bike lay crumpled next to him. Fresh blood dripped down the boy's forehead and he struggled to catch his breath.

I walked toward the crowd with Stephen in his wheelchair. A twinge of emotion sent a tremble through me as I paused. My hesitation quickly deteriorated at the sight of this little boy's eyes. "Do you need help?" I asked. "I'm a nurse. Do you want my help?" I asked the row-mover.

"Yes, hurry, he's bleeding. He's hurt real bad. Hurry!" The cloak of ignorance and ill-suited fear fell away with common need.

His son did all right. The police came a few minutes later and complimented "the care done at the scene." The little boy's artery had been severed and he could have lost "too much blood."

The row-mover and I became friends. The next few years we volunteered at grade schools and high schools teaching HIV awareness. We named the talk "The Row-Mover." He believed that "increasing the public's knowledge about HIV would move people to a more therapeutic view of life where they could deal realistically with their limitations."

~~~

Michael still stood at Stephen's bedside. He wanted his friend to wake up, but knew that sleep was important for his ailing body. "Chris, what are you going to do?" Michael asked. "It's almost time for trick-or-treating."

Seeing Michael touch Stephen's Halloween costume, I realized another holiday might come and go without our possible involvement. I decided to change what we could. "Michael, how about us bringing Halloween to Stephen?"

The next two hours, Michael and I decorated Stephen's

room. We moved his bed closer to the front door so he could hear the other children as they asked for treats. Mirrors were strategically positioned to reflect the ghosts and goblins that waited at the front door. Streamers in orange, brown and green flowed down from the ceiling. Orange and white mini-lights were intertwined with plastic spiders and rubber snakes. Stephen's face was painted an awful green, appropriate for ET, while he remained asleep. The oxcimeter probe on his finger created the final ET touch. Pumpkins with happy faces were lit by small candles. The oxygen tanks were wrapped in aluminum foil resembling R2D2. Obewankanobe laser-sword stickers pointed to a sign that said, "May the force be with you." Eerie music played in the background. Stephen slept.

As nighttime approached, Michael's mother came to retrieve him. It was time to get ready for the evening's adventure. As Michael showed her his handiwork she giggled with delight. In her arms she carried Michael's sister, a wondrous trophy of God's handiwork.

~~~

A few months previous, Michael's mother had come to my house in desperation. Her husband being out of town, she shared with me the terrible news that her pregnancy was in jeopardy. She had been having contractions and was bleeding. The doctor had been unable to give her medication to stop the premature labor due to her "unusual allergy."

She now wept, "What kind of a person am I to save my life and put my child in danger?" Her deep sadness was overwhelming.

The doctor had left her with, "It's in God's hands now. We will have to wait and see." The familiar dance of wait. People from all walks of life have to dance with rocks in their shoes to this dance of wait. Now my friend would have to.

The only thing I could offer was to dance with her. Many times before when Stephen's life had hung suspended in the space between life and death, we had had someone—friend or stranger—to dance with us.

Needing to prepare some medication, I placed Stephen next to her on the couch. As her feet rested on our giant, over-stuffed "cow" footstool, she leaned back and touched Stephen's hair as his head rested in her lap. She reached outside her grief and despair to comfort my child, when only an inch away her own unborn child fought for life.

Having finished preparing the next medicine, I came back to the living room. There on the couch lay my son, his hand gently touching my friend's round belly. Her hand was positioned over his. She was asleep. Stephen laid quietly smiling. This gentle, touching scene continued for another hour. Peace.

An unborn child was resting in the hands of the Almighty. My friend was sleeping on angel wings. Stephen—his temple riddled with disability and disease, his soul pure and holy—was once again the tool of the Creator.

Four months later Michael's sister was born, perfect in every way.

~~~

Michael had hurried home to put on his costume while Stephen slept. The first batch of trick-or-treaters came, then the second. Soon word got out in the neighborhood that Stephen's house looked pretty cool.

Eddy and his science-fair team stood at the door. They—along with their brothers, sisters and parents—all approached

Stephen's house together. Stephen was awake when they came and was moving with delight at the sound of their voices. After obtaining permission from their parents, the gang came into the house to see Stephen. They had been missing him at school.

Soon Stephen had six costumed buddies jumping all over his bed, their parents and siblings looking on. The doorbell rang and someone would yell, "Come on in!" At one time I counted thirty-two masked people joining the celebration and giving Stephen low-fives. Their interactions with Stephen flowed without encumbrance; Eddy's group moved freely around Stephen's room, demonstrating for their parents how each piece of medical equipment worked. The last family left for home about 11:30 p.m. We hadn't missed Halloween. Like so much else in life, it had come to us.

~~~

Monday morning back at school, Mrs. Rooney's class worked feverishly to finish up the science projects. Tomorrow night the fair would commence. Eddy's group hastened to prepare posters, finishing the last promising touches.

"Stephen, whatever you do, don't get sick tomorrow night. You just have to be there!" were Eddy's final instructions.

After weeks of preparation, the science fair began. All of the teammates in Mrs. Rooney's class were present and accounted for, Stephen included. Eddy's group stood in a circle around him. Many inquisitive students wanted to know why their display table had been moved out of the room. What could they possibly do without a display table? Gathered around Stephen, they politely awaited their turn in the competition.

"Now, last but not least, we are happy to present team

number four," announced Mrs. Rooney.

Strategically, Eddy's group parted, standing in straight rows beside Stephen's wheelchair. When they parted, beeping, blinking monitors were visible. Oxygen tanks stood behind them, still dressed like R2D2. Janie began. "The advances in electricity have helped our friend Stephen live at home." She looked at Stephen and smiled as he basked in her attention. "We will show you tonight how these machines, all powered by electricity, work together to help Stephen. First, however, we would like to share with you some facts. One out of every five Americans has some form of disability. Many of them require some sort of electrical assistance. Our bodies have been designed to work together. Sometimes we need help to keep everything working together."

Concluding her portion, she added, "Each one of us may need the help of one of these machines sometime in our life. We may need surgery, get cancer, or may have an accident. None of us can predict what might happen to us in the future. So all of us are the same. We all need each other." A hesitant applause ruffled the silence.

Next it was Jason and Jerry's turn. "This is R2D2 and these are his robot friends." They talked about Stephen's oxygen equipment and displayed the machines, pushing in knobs and buttons to show everyone how they worked. "This is Chewbakka the c-pap machine, and this is Princess Leah the LP10 ventilator. This is Oliver the oxcimeter," Jerry said, introducing the machines like old friends. He proudly showed how the medical machines worked and how the alarms were set.

Jason removed a mitten that had been placed on Stephen's hand and unveiled the "ET finger." He continued to explain its light readings, and ended their portion with, ". . . and may the force be with you." Next Connie and Lisa demonstrated "'Vicki vacuums and Sister Sally suction" machines. They showed everyone how to suction someone's airway by using a glass with tinted pink water. The *Sluurrpppp* noise make Stephen laugh. Soon the whole group was laughing and giggling. Eddy's team's families had joined the laughter. Some families and peers looked on with disgust and frowns on their faces.

Eddy regained control of the group. "Attention, please. Attention!" His persistent voice quieted the crowd. He walked to Stephen's side and held his hand. "This is my friend Stephen. He comes to school and lives in our neighborhood because of the advances in electricity. Scientists will continue to improve machines that help people with disabilities. We have to help each other to see past the machines and meet the people they help. That is one thing that electricity can't do for us.

"I didn't like Stephen when the school year started. All I saw was all this stuff," he said, pointing to the machines. "Now I see Stephen, and he is my friend." Feeling a bit uneasy surround-ed by the room's awkward silence, he turned to the members in his team who stood proudly around and behind Stephen and said, "We have to talk for Stephen. It's up to us. Some of those guys just don't get it."

In Chinese calligraphy,
the word for crisis is written
by joining the symbols
for danger
and
opportunity.

Bellyache Blues

Pulling back the sheer curtains and opening the window, I was greeted by the warm breeze of a new summer day. Just months ago the snow had piled high along the sidewalk and the frost had created a frozen crust on the ground. The winter's frigid silence had now conceded temporary defeat, giving way to fragrant flowers and soft ground. Gazing upon the luscious green grass, I wrapped myself in Earth's life-giving grace.

Three months earlier, Stephen and I had made a another journey to Children's Hospital. Embarking upon one of our lives' most challenging paths, we made our way to the experts. The air then had been bitterly cold and its arctic crunch was heard under my feet as I carried Stephen to the van.

I had exhausted every trick, remedy, idea, and suggestion I knew to ease his pain. It hadn't worked. The best of my abilities and the abilities of the doctors and nurses in our hometown had come up short.

So many times Stephen had remained home to get better. This time was different. He hurt too much. We traveled forty miles to Children's Hospital in downtown Chicago where Stephen was admitted to the Pediatric ICU. In the hospital, weeks of IV antibiotics wrestled with the infection in his blood-stream, finally ridding him of most of the bacteria. Still, his health declined. His body rejected the IV food and fluid it needed to survive. I continued to try and comfort the shell that housed my beautiful boy, who now appeared emaciated, yellow and weak.

Through all of the tests, procedures and many different caregivers, he still managed to smile for us. Often I rested in his embrace to soothe my fears, my aloneness, my grief. Nights and days repeated themselves until time knew no schedule. The lights of the ICU, the sounds of the life-giving machines— all kept going like a grandfather clock that needed no winding.

Now it was spring and an oriole stopped to drink from the sweet nectar that hung outside my room at the Ronald McDonald House. Today my son would move from the ICU to a rehabilitation unit where he would, hopefully, grow stronger and I would learn his new life-sustaining machines. It had been eighty-seven days since the snow covered the earth when we began our sojourn here.

~~~

Midpoint in that sojourn, Stephen's health had declined; death was imminent. The medical experts and myself were brought together in an emergency "brainstorming session." His body had been rejecting IV food, antibiotics and fluid. That, and his increased abdominal pain, signaled a definite problem in his belly. His pediatric surgeon was called to consult with the other medical experts.

Months before, during a previous clinic appointment, she had informed me, "You will know when you need my help. When that time comes, I will do the best that I can to help you and your son." Her time had come.

Upon her arrival she sat with medical students, the residents and nurses caring for Stephen, myself and one of the hospital chaplains. "Stephen's condition has deteriorated to the point where he will not live much longer if we do not try to intervene surgically. The tests we have done do not show any conclusive findings. However, there is something going on in his belly. We need to find out what it is and fix it if we can. I'm sorry but I don't have any other suggestions. He is weak, very weak. His chances of surviving the trauma of anesthesia and the surgery itself are low. I would estimate twenty percent chance that he would survive the surgery and post-surgical healing. If we do not perform the surgery, he will live a few more days—maybe. The decision is up to you. He sure loves life, even now. He's got that going for him. Remember that, and I will check back with you in an hour."

I remember sitting in the rocking chair, tangled in tubes and wires, gently rocking Stephen. He had a 1-1 nurse, which was somewhat unusual even in the ICU. We ducked and tried to keep out of each other's way as numerous medications and cares were performed.

I rocked back and forth. I closed my eyes and touched his face, putting to memory every line, indentation and form. I wanted to remember how his face looked when I couldn't see it any longer. I wanted to trace his face when he was no longer in my arms. I was touching the essence of beauty itself. The origin of joy. Stephen dissolved in my arms, molding to fit my curves as we continued to rock back and forth.

A cuckoo clock had been brought into the room by one of the volunteers. The constant *ticktock* kept time to the rhythmic rocking. Stephen slept in my arms. As long as I held him, touched him or sang to him, he rested. Sleep wasn't a normal nightly thing for caregivers in the ICU. Sleep was a precious commodity, put on hold for another time and place. We often spoke of a whole night's sleep and grinned at its fading remembrance.

Dr. R returned alone and stood in front of me in the rocking chair. She pulled up a stool and greeted us like someone looking at a new painting in a museum. Not saying a word to me, she asked for Stephen's chart. She wrote pre-op orders, lifted up the red flag announcing new medical orders and handed them to Stephen's nurse. The nurse read the orders. "You have decided to go ahead and have surgery. I will get him ready."

Dr. R stood up, put both hands on the armrests of the rocking chair and looked deeply into my eyes. "I will do everything I can to preserve this beautiful picture. With your permission, I will do my best. How's tomorrow morning?"

Still not saying a word, I nodded Yes. Stephen had helped me to pass all fear and grief. Even more, he had given strength and confidence to all in his presence.

~~~

The oriole had left the feeder and my eyes had been drawn to the fuzzy canine outside, running and bouncing after his big red ball. The managers of the Ronald McDonald house played with him every day at this same time. The night before Stephen's surgery, the dog—Harry—was lying by the door to my room. On his collar was a note. "I'm your delivery dog. Dinner is in the refrigerator. Please look after me until morning when my owners will return. If you need to go back to the hospital just call them and they will come and get me."

Harry laid on my feet as I sat and ate some of my favorite foods: turkey, mashed potatoes, cranberries, and pumpkin pie. Later we slept together on Harry's blanket. Petting his soft fur and listening to his rhythmic breathing lulled my anxious soul to sleep.

The Ronald McDonald house is a respite in a dreary land

for wayfaring pilgrims. Many times the road to recovery or transition to death finalizes itself inside nearby hospital walls. Flowers, wooden floors, bookshelves lined with good reads, newspapers, fresh coffee, Easter baskets and Christmas trees grace this real home. Volunteers make Sunday dinner; others bring fresh cookies or replenish the bathrooms with soap, toothbrushes, toothpaste. Bedrooms are comforting with hand-made quilts, pictures and homemade artwork.

As I and others rested, ate, bathed, read or tried to sleep, the fragrance of previous caregivers' tears blessed us. The prayers of mothers, fathers, brothers, sisters, and volunteers cushioned our aching hearts—our oasis in the desert of loss.

Making my bed and choosing only twice-worn clothes, I grabbed a cup of coffee and headed to the hospital. Church bells greeted me every morning signifying the beginning of the early morning service. I smiled and waved to the familiar people entering the church for mass. The church's stained glass back wall was vibrant in the sunlight. The mist on the grass cloaked the ground. The church's high steeple rose to the low clouds and its bells' melodious tune was heard, not seen. All welcomed the day invisibly.

The old man and his old dog were walking to my right just as they had every morning for eighty-seven days since the Ronald McDonald House had become my home. They both showed life's time. His stature was crooked and stooped forward, silver hair glowing in the sunlight. The red leash in his hand held a small graying dog. The two walked hunched over. Every morning I would wave and greet them, but age and fear didn't allow them to answer back.

"Oh no!" I shouted. "Stop!!"

I dropped my bag and ran toward the dog. The old man was walking as fast as he could toward the dog. He had accidentally dropped the leash. A car was coming down the street, headed directly toward the dog. I screamed for the car to stop, while waving my arms violently. How could this happen?

I was close enough to the man to see the horror in his panicked face. I ran down the middle of the street toward the oncoming car. Still it came.

"STOP!"

The car was coming closer to the dog. Maybe he saw me, but the driver hadn't slowed. The dog was going to be hit. The old dog didn't hear me either. This man's life, his most tender possession, was about to be snuffed.

Suddenly from between two parked cars, another dog ran into the street. He came between the oncoming car and the old dog. *AAHHHH*—now both dogs were in trouble.

"Wait! Stopppppppp . . .." The car's brakes screeched. And then, a terrible thud.

The old man picked up his dog who lay untouched but cowering and shaking in the middle of the street. He slowly reached down and touched the brave dog who had run out between the oncoming car and his dog. The dog silently got up and walked away.

I finally reached the old man and helped him and his dog back to his house. This time the old man spoke: "Come in honey, sit for a minute. I'll get you a cup of cold water." Still trembling, I agreed and followed him onto his porch. Stopping to pet his old dog first, the man then brought me a cup of water. He looked at me and said, "You stay here with Barney. I'm going to find the other dog and make sure he's okay. He got hit pretty hard by the car. He saved my Barney. I have to find him. It's the least I can do."

As the old man got to the squeaky porch door, he looked back at me petting Barney and said, "It won't be hard to find him. I saw his collar. I'll call him and he'll come to me. His name is Shadrack Josiah."

I felt lightheaded and had to sit on the floor. The man came back and stood over me. "Honey, what's the matter?"

I held his hand. "It's okay, mister. You don't have to go find the dog. That was my Shadrack Josiah. He died two years ago."

We sat on the porch steps and shared a vial of time. "Angel dog," he repeated, over and over again. "The angel dog saved my Barney."

I continued to the hospital, walking considerably lighter. My dog—an angel dog. On this Earth we had walked together for sixteen years. Now he was an angel dog. His spirit continued to bring help and joy here, now. How I longed to hold him, see him, play with him. How privileged I was to have seen him again.

I arrived at Stephen's room still vibrating from the experience. The nurses thought I was nervous about Stephen's surgery, but time did not present itself with even a minute to explain. Two new children had been brought into the ICU, utilizing all the resources the unit could manage.

It was 7:30 a.m., time for Stephen to go to surgery. I kissed him and told him of the "angel dog." He smiled. Outside the surgery room, Dr. R introduced me to the other doctors and residents who would be assisting her. Some of them looked over Stephen's chart, shaking their heads in disbelief that this critical boy was to be operated on. Dr. R asked me if I had any questions. Not having had a chance to prepare since this morning's encounter, I spoke: "Stephen and I want to thank you for the opportunity to help him live without pain. I just want you to know that God holds the big picture in the palm of His hand and He will help you today. Whatever the outcome, thank you."

Surprised and silent, they took Stephen, my precious child, behind the operating room doors.

Dr. R returned to the Surgical Waiting Room after eight hours of surgery on Stephen. "Chris, you will never believe what I found. Usually we cut pretty deep when we enter the abdomen. This time I cut just through the skin, and it's a good thing I did because his liver was right there. Had I cut as deep as I usually do I would have cut his liver and he would have hemorrhaged. His diaphragm ruptured, his stomach was up in his chest cavity through the hole in his diaphragm. The liver took over all the space in his abdomen and adhered to the wall of the peritoneum. We had to patch the hole in his diaphragm and repair the ducts between the liver and surrounding organs that got stretched. His trachea has a small patch, too, where the top of the stomach adhered to the trachea and the aorta. Remarkably, he is doing quite well. They are closing now. We will move him to ICU in a few minutes. I can't believe how much pain he must have had."

Thirty more days in the Intensive Care Unit were then devoted to healing Stephen and combatting complications. Finally, we moved to the unit from which Stephen would be discharged. This was the last step before home. I would learn the ventilator, Stephen's new cares, a new nursing service would be hired, nurses would be trained, medications and supplies ordered and received—and we would go home.

Stephen's belongings and medical equipment were all packed up. Stephen was graduating from the ICU. He had survived, defying death another time. His life has a purpose and he would continue here on this Earth—in this body—until his purpose had been served. Proud, I wheeled the bed as we headed out of ICU into the hall that would lead us to home's familiar welcome.

Once outside the door, Dr. N motioned for us to return. Puzzled, I turned the heavy cargo around and went back to the ICU. Dr. N smiled and said, "You forgot something."

She led us to the bell, tears of joy streaming down both our faces. Two of the residents who had helped us through Stephen's disease propped us up. I took Stephen's hand and, together, we rang the bell. The nurses, doctors and families shattered ICU's artificial quietude with applause and cheers of "Well done! All right!" The ring of hope and survival stayed with us as we left. It tolled hope for the many who clung to life. We were headed for our safe harbor.

The bell had been donated to the ICU. It had been used on a ship. When a great storm occurred at sea, many on land worried that the ship might return empty, silent, without survivors. As the ship would meet land, any survivor would ring the bell. The townspeople would run to greet the ship in celebration, to welcome all who had returned.

*A*nd when your children's children
shall think themselves alone
in the fields, the store, the shops,
upon the highway,
or in the silence
of the pathless woods,
they will not be alone.

Chief Seattle (1855)

Spirit Medicine

Stephen looked adorable in his light rose-colored ribbon shirt. One of his regular night nurses had made it for him, his very own Indian dress shirt. Rose and teal ribbons flowed from its long sleeves, creating a trail of rainbows when he moved his arms. All evidence of his physical disabilities was lost in the beauty of his radiant expression when he wore this shirt. On this day, we would ride with Ed, the medicine man, and his family to the powwow, and the awkward limitations of Stephen's physical disabilities would disappear in this proud celebration of ancestral heritage.

Culture was important in our lives, and we shared hours of exploration into his Native American heritage. The powwow was an expression of life, filled with color and movement. I was determined to escort Stephen to all of the Indian events, ceremonies and activities that I could find. He was born Native American and we would live in its beautiful reflection.

Stephen had been loved by his biological family, yet they had been unable to care for him personally. The best they could do was to pray that God, the Great Spirit, would connect Stephen with one who would walk by his side on his journey. I exchanged my life of being single and unencumbered to walk with this child. But we had already been joined before time as we know it existed. Indian ways effortlessly reconnected us.

Stephen first took part in a powwow after he had come home to live with me. Most of his doctors thought I was crazy for even thinking about taking Stephen somewhere loud. In those younger years, Stephen was easily startled by loud nois-es. The slam of a door or the random clapping of hands would cause waves of trembling, and his body would stiffen. In prepa-ration for Stephen's first powwow, medications were readied to intervene, should his body's homeostasis be challenged. Emergency procedures and protocols were practiced before our arrival at the high school where the powwow was to be held.

To Stephen and me, at that first powwow, everything was new. Large drums sat on the floor in each of the four corners of the room. One drum sat on the floor in the center. Each drum was surrounded by men who sat holding large drumsticks. Encircling them, men, women and children created individual clusters. Each circle mirrored individual family traditions evi-denced by their attire. Some wore deerskin, others jingle dress-es or feathers surrounded by beads and jewels.

Stephen sat on my lap on the gymnasium floor. We used the wall for support. We were new in the neighborhood and didn't know anyone, so we sat alone. It was quiet. After a brief intro-duction the drumming began. It was loud. All five drums began to beat the same rhythm at the same time without any cue.

The booms reverberated throughout the room. I was stunned and I looked quickly at Stephen as I reached for the emergency bag. Without question, if the music affected me to this degree, Stephen's body—which shuddered at the slightest sound—would need intervention for stabilization. I looked at Stephen's face as the drums drilled through my ears. He was laughing. The sweet awesome laugh that shook his whole body. I had witnessed this laugh before, the night that I dropped the tray leaving Stephen's hospital room. I touched him as the beats of the drums reacquainted themselves with our wandering souls. Gazing up from Stephen's face I became aware of swirling gowns, colorful headpieces and tapping feet. We sat transformed by this picture that animated love and dignity. Stephen was not afraid of this "noise." We came home to the drums that day.

Some time later, when Stephen had been deathly ill in the hospital before Christmas, I had called my friend Pat to ask for help. Pat and I had both cared for special-needs children in foster care and she had become my close friend. Her husband was Native American and had helped Stephen and me connect with the American Indian community. Ed, the medicine man, had first come to Stephen at Pat's request. She had told him, "My friend Chrissy's on the phone and she won't stop calling me until I get someone to go to the hospital and pray with her son."

Sometimes "Indian time" and my normal hyper-speed clashed. This was one of those times. Stephen was near death in a hospital bed. If there was some type of ceremony or ritual that needed to be performed before Stephen made the transition to the next world, it was my responsibility to find him the guide.

Ed eventually arrived at the hospital and was escorted to the Intensive Care Unit and Stephen. It was late in the evening and night rounds were complete. Stephen's nurse sat in the doorway of his room. Ed reached over and gave me a big hug. I sobbed in his arms as he held me. I had been holding Stephen for hours and now this strong man comforted me.

"You are brave," he said. I told him about Stephen and that the medical efforts to correct Stephen's condition were failing. He repeated, "You are very brave." He began to chant and bless my little boy. He circled Stephen's bed a few times, then paused at his feet. He took sweet grass and sage, braided them together with a lock of my hair and lit them on fire.

A very small fire . . . in the Intensive Care Unit . . . in the hospital. Stephen was soothed by the song and the smoke that rose to meet the generations of ancestors in the sky. However, as the smoke transcended to the sky it passed over the smoke detectors. I cradled Stephen in my arms as the fire alarms blared. The sprinklers soon emitted a soft spray, saturating everything. I laughed so hard that Stephen awoke, setting equipment alarms off in tune to the fire alarms. The fire doors slammed shut and water kept squirting from the ceiling.

Ed left. Stephen and I laughed until we cried and thankfully so did his nurses, the doctors and the firemen. Many of them shook their heads in disbelief. Not one of them remembered anything about our visitor that night. "Just pray, no props," had been our admonishment.

Now, some years later, we loaded Stephen's medical necessities into the car and rode to a powwow with Ed. We arrived a little late. Dancers were already swaying and tapping to the drums and chants. Stephen rode in his wagon propped up with pillows. He wore his new Indian ribbon shirt. Many children and teachers surrounded Stephen as he entered the room. We were not strangers anymore. One of the boys grabbed Stephen's wagon handle and pulled him around to the center of the room. The children swarmed over Stephen. I watched as the circle of friends rotated around the room. When the music stopped, the children brought Stephen back to me.

The announcer said, "Today we have a special surprise for all of you. We are going to honor a boy and his mother who overcome more difficulties in one day then most of us will in a lifetime." I looked around the room to determine who this surprise was for. The announcer continued, "Stephen and Chris, please come to the center of the circle."

A round of applause filled the room. I was stunned. Ed walked over to me, helped me off the floor and carried Stephen to the center of the circle. One of Stephen's little friends carried his oxygen. We sat next to the center drum in the middle of the floor. Stephen sat Indian-style on my lap.

"Today we honor you. We give thanks to the Great Spirit for your willingness to walk this road. We dance in your presence that our feet may become strong and walk bravely as you do." Silence filled the room. If tears made noise, mine would have sounded like driving rain on a glassy lake. The drums began. All of them beat the same rhythm at the same moment. The singers began to sing and dancers flowed to the music. Stephen and I gazed upon this vision, capturing its essence in our memories. The dance crescendoed, filling the room with a frenzy of activity made of energy itself.

Suddenly, the electrical power failed. Silence. Blackness. The drums stopped, the dancers froze like statues, no one breathed. In absolute darkness, the drums began again—inexplicably, all of them at the precise same moment. The beat of the drum, heard and not seen, permeated our souls. No prejudice or question survived the silent darkness. Peace and unity lived. Soon tapping of feet was heard. Movement was felt, not seen. Stephen and I sat entranced by the sheer energy of life.

The electricity came back on. It lit a room of dancers and drummers all twirling around us, music and movement made perfect in silence, the rhythm purified by energy in darkness.

A Child of Mine

"I'll lend you a little time, a child of mine," He said,
"For you to love while he lives, and mourn when he is dead.

"It may be six or seven years, or twenty-two or -three,
but will you, till I call him back, take care of him for me?

"He'll bring charms to gladden you, and shall his stay be brief,
You'll have his lovely memories as solace for your grief.

"I cannot promise he will stay, since all from earth return,
But there are lessons taught down there, I want this child to learn.

"I've looked the wide world over in my search for teachers true,
And from the throngs that crowd life's lanes, I have selected you.

"Now will you give him all your love, not think the labor vain,
Nor hate me when I come to call to take him back again."

We'll shelter him with tenderness, we'll love him while we may;
And for the happiness we've known, will ever grateful stay.

But shall the angels call for him much sooner then we planned,
We'll brave the bitter grief that comes, and try to understand!

Author unknown

Angel Nikes

I hurt. With every breath I took, I ached. Somewhere down deep inside me, the substance intended to connect my soul to my physical being had come unglued. Senses had heightened and with every struggling breath that Stephen took, the glue came more undone. My soul wanted to run and play in a sun-filled field of yellow daffodils, like a child newly discovering nature. I wanted to rid myself of all time—and of all pain. Violent sobs had drained my body's energy, tears glazed my eyes. Every muscle had twitched to sleep and my bones lay heavy under my skin, nerves exposed and constantly scraped by grief and pain.

Stephen struggled to breathe. Pneumonia had captured his body. He used all his energy to pull air into his swollen lungs and with all his strength he tried to force it out again. Over and over his chest rose and fell sounding like a clogged and rusted pipe. The rhythmic patting of my hands on his chest to open his fragile airways beat in tune with every agonizing breath.

It had been many hours since the doctor called bearing con-solation and kindness instead of hoped-for orders and treat-ment. The hospice nurse was gone, too, leaving her prayer echoing, detached words that bounced about the room. The nurse who was to bring relief had been delayed. Minutes ticked slowly by, keeping rhythm with my pounding head.

The walls of Stephen's cheerful bedroom seemed like a shrinking steel tomb. I had held my faith tenderly, as in a glass box perched high on a bookshelf. It now teetered close to the edge as I whispered a prayer that it would not fall and shatter.

Stephen's blink caught my eye as his soul met mine. With military-like attention, I waited to respond. I would help him as long as he fought to live in his body. Both of our bodies now trembled. His eyes looked toward his tape recorder and then quickly at me. Stephen's "eye sign" for "sing." Oh my God, he wanted me to sing! How could I bury the sobs that wracked my body? I couldn't move. My body parts were frozen in a kneeling position by the side of his bed. It had been my position for the last four hours. Whenever my touch left his body, he struggled harder to breathe. His body's temperature soared with every muscle that moved to regain my contact.

My bladder was full, my head pounded, I was thirsty. I did not even know if I had another breath to breathe myself. Somehow, softly, I began to hum, "Jesus loves me . . .." Suddenly a calm presence filled the air. It permeated every one of my disconnected cells. Peace filled the room. I looked at Stephen. Certainly he was dying. This presence had come to make his body whole. He would be able to walk, run, breathe without effort, sing, and return hug's embrace. Peace so great is only possible in the Almighty's presence. Stephen was going home. I could move. I got up, still patting Stephen and still singing softly.

The room filled with a haze. A glimmer of light appeared by the window. The light's brightness was blinding and my hand, for the first time, left Stephen to shield my eyes. I knew that Stephen's body was completing its transition from this world to the next. The haze inside the room thickened, creating a shield from the blinding white light. We were enveloped in this light.

I was puzzled by this encounter but not afraid. Every breath brought strength and courage. I could sing, "Jesus never fails, Jesus never fails, heaven and Earth may pass away but Jesus never fails." The fog continued to shelter us from the light in the window as other small light particles floated into the room. No fixtures, no walls, no furniture seemed to exist—only space and time. Brightness from beyond continued to increase until I touched my eyes to see if they had been burned. I felt no heat.

Stephen's breathing was easier now. The light from beyond the window had filtered though the haze that sheltered us like a river on air. Every particle that danced around us brought life. We were standing on holy ground. Pain, despair, grief, hurt did not exist. They were gone. Stephen's eyes were open and moving the same way that he followed me when I walked about his room. Peace graced his face. He knew this presence. His body rested in this familiar serenity.

The light particles in the fog began to connect, forming an angelic being. She stood tall, with arms held high to her side, shielding us from the source of light behind her. The light was a part of her. Time had stopped—there was only eternity. I held my arms out in front of me, offering my son to this being of light. I thanked her for being with us and shielding us from the consuming light.

The brightness began to dim, the fog separated. Stephen was still here, on this Earth, in this body. I could feel his skin cool and his chest rise and fall without struggle. Stephen knew that to extend ourselves in praise to God when we have nothing left would summon help from heaven. As I looked at my son, and touched his feet and ankles that still glowed with the light, I smiled and said, "Angel Nikes." Stephen was ready to run in heaven.

They that wait upon the Lord shall renew their strength; they shall mount up with wings as eagles; they shall run, and not be weary; and they shall walk, and not faint.

Isaiah 40:31

Broken Promises, Broken Dreams

During the last forty-eight hours, Stephen had only slept for an intermittent hour or two. His stomach hurt. Three days before, we had sat at Chicago Children's Hospital and Clinic, attempting to discover a way to ease his pain. Now we struggled with man's shortcomings once again.

The television news talked of millions of dollars used for different political programs and political figures' salaries. Income taxes rose, the cost of living went up, and medical care declined. Money continued to be taken from medical research and direct medical care and allocated to the defense industry. Decisive political figures continued to allocate money to militarily maintain a safe haven for our sick bodies to inhabit.

Material possessions and luxurious trinkets become meaningless, however, upon hearing the words *cancer, emphysema, paralysis*, and the like. Sometimes we are reminded that medical compromise happens to all of us when a celebrity is suddenly struck with a life-shattering disability. Sometimes a famous person reveals an illness, allowing us to deal second-handedly with these issues. Often we make wrong choices that further injure our health. Rarely do we contribute to organizations that assist in medical advances. Always we expect medical treatment for our ailing bodies.

Stephen lay hurting, his body suffering. Moving Stephen very delicately to prevent him from further hurt, I wondered if some of that money could have found a cure for one of his diseases if it had been given to research. Realizing that I must "change what I can," I continued to get Stephen dressed.

The medical experts had offered no other suggestions to minimize the pain left by a fistula in Stephen's stomach. The progressive deterioration in his lungs had disallowed him from surgical repair. His body would be compromised by the anesthesia and surgery more then his pain and discomfort. I tried to spit out the bitter taste that was left by the words: "He is not a surgical candidate. His body will have to take care of itself. It may get better and it might get worse."

The suffering of children is difficult to transform into something good. We have to accept it by faith; accept and keep going. That day it was more difficult than most.

Stephen had been home from the hospital for a few months following the surgery to repair his ruptured diaphragm. His level of care had increased greatly. Nurses were few and far between. The time spent teaching the new caregivers his advanced treatments and directly caring for Stephen had begun to take its toll on my health.

Also during the time of Stephen's recent hospitalization, the marriage that I had clung to so desperately began to fail. In 1989 when I had brought Stephen home, I had doubted I would ever marry. It was a difficult decision. I didn't know if I would have enough energy for both a full-time needy child and a man-woman relationship. Stephen's life and the lives of others that would come after him would be my life. I made a choice. A deliberate choice.

My courtship and eventual marriage, however, had been a fairy-tale princess story for me. Swept off my feet by my Prince Charming, I reveled in the time and attention that he gave me. Life was, for a time, all I had ever dreamed it could be. I had a husband I was so proud of and we had our wonderful son—my dream of a family complete.

Stephen and I would leave our homeland to be with my husband in Chicago, leaving my family and support system for my "real" family. We had been married two years, however, before we could live together. State and federal health-care regulations prohibited us from moving Stephen from Minnesota to Illinois until all the paperwork and clearances had been approved. It took two very long years.

A time eventually came, however, when I had to admit I was too tired for all of it. I struggled with the reality of a disintegrating marriage and my decision to care for needy children. My doctor explained my inability to feel rested. "You've used your body up. Plain and simple, you have used it all up. It has taken years to get this way, and it will take years to get back what you have lost—years." I looked for the quick fix: "Give me a pill and I'll keep going." It worked—for a short time.

I tried to get respite help for Stephen, but extra hours of nursing care were not granted because this was my illness, not Stephen's. I even solicited funds from people. Having secured promises from some to help care financially for Stephen while I recovered, I ran head-first into the fact that I could not use their help. If I accepted their money now, Stephen would no longer be eligible for his government aid. Private financial assistance would help us short-term, but when the crisis was over he would no longer have the waiver in place to care for his nursing at home. We were stuck, entangled in rules, regulations and nights of unrest.

Stephen was hospitalized during this time for pneumonia. Intravenous antibiotics, continuous lung medication and increased ventilator settings increased Stephen's level of medical care even more. The realization that Stephen was gravely ill and that I could burn out created a surreal world. I robotically had been performing tasks for years without proper sleep and nourishment. How could my body give up on me now?

In the hospital, Stephen's pneumonia improved. His papa helped him recover. The only papa Stephen had ever known, my husband, was struggling, too, with life's unfairness and human limits. I wasn't able to be there for either of them.

Years ago I had brought this little boy from the hospital to care for him in my home: a house with warm walls, smells of freshly-baked chocolate-chip cookies, doorbells, and company; a safe place where he could be cared for by the same people, not many different hands—loving, caring, family who would get to know Stephen and maintain an environment in which he could safely thrive.

Now I was afraid that I was too tired to bring him home. Stephen's papa was tired, too. His business had been put on hold many times to handle Stephen's medical crises. Family and social contacts had become minimal. Just not enough time.

Stephen would not be allowed to stay in the hospital to recover. The hospital directors needed to "clamp down on abusive admissions." This was my crisis, I was told repeatedly, not Stephen's. Extensive talks didn't stop the arrows that flew by, hurting us. Stephen would be hurt. He would have to be placed in an institution. My promise to Stephen was being broken and when it broke, I broke too.

Stephen was admitted to an interim facility. There he would continue his life. His body would continue to be treated for pneumonia with IV antibiotics. The ventilator supplied adequate oxygen to his tiring lungs. The only way I could continue caring for Stephen was to face my fears, accept my limits and find him the best care that could be provided within the confines of medical and governmental restrictions.

Hours of preparation and copious paperwork outlined his history and current treatment plan. Upon arrival at the new facility, I sought solace for my soul that was not found. Maybe I could find solace for Stephen. Many children lived there. Their lives swung like hammocks in the unpredictable wind— the winds of family turmoil, exhausted parents and caregivers—vulnerable to governmental choices and political budget cuts that rained daily upon them. They were all the victims of human limitation.

In the facilities where special-needs children are cared for by loving, skilled and generous people, these trained professionals have confronted the limits and changed what they could. But they are not able to change the dynamics of families that hurt; they cannot make political agents design programs that embrace investment in a disabled child. They cannot ease the pain of separation for a mother who leaves her son in their care as she returns to save her marriage or her job. They cannot change the many variables that landed the children in their facility. Daily, with love and compassion, they transform anger into glorious, tender care of the children left behind.

Now my son, my joy, lay in this institution.

The facility housed a small chapel, adorned by an old wooden cross. Stephen and I stopped there before I left him in the hands that represented all that I had rescued him from. The hands that signified my broken promise. We paused at the foot of the wooden cross: "God, if there is a God, have mercy on us and hear our prayer." The glass box of faith that contained my beliefs shattered onto the floor below. I surrounded Stephen with his personal belongings, kissed him gently, and prayed that his Auntie Valerie would forgive me. I turned and walked out of the building. Alone, I thought.

Learning how to rest myself was very difficult. Many times I would visit and care for Stephen. When nighttime came the impending separation became unendurable. Often my violent sobs affected my ability to drive. Somehow I made it home. Hours later I would return.

One day Stephen had been experiencing pain. His ear was infected and the visiting doctor debrided his ear without giving Stephen any anesthesia or pain medications. I was told, "The doctor didn't feel it was necessary to give any medication for pain, as the procedure would only take a minute of two." Then the nurse added, "Your son didn't say anything." UGH! I wanted to run out of that place with Stephen and hide. I wanted to protect him from the demons of silent sponges, those who take advantage of children because they cannot cry out loud.

Stephen finally rested and was asleep. I tried to soothe his bleeding ear and his hurt. I felt as though all my nerves were outside my skin. The institution had rules and unless Stephen was physically in crisis, by their determination, I could not stay overnight. Pain, tears, discomfort were not enough to bend the rules.

How could I leave my son? The turmoil of my soul was unimaginable. I placed Stephen in his bed, bathed him, caressed him, and prayed that he would somehow be comforted after I left. I kissed him and turned away.

Just outside of the doorway I paused to look back at

Stephen. A familiar yet fresh presence filled the air. My grief was swallowed up in its fullness. Sitting in the rocking chair was an older Native American woman. She was knitting and rocking back and forth. A white quilt lay on her lap ready to hold Stephen when he awoke. On Stephen's bed sat two children—an Indian boy and girl. They were playing a game and singing. I saw Stephen looking at them as I had seen him look many times before. Then I thought he was just blankly staring—now I saw what he did. I smiled and felt lightened.

A few more steps toward the door I glanced back again. At the entrance to Stephen's room stood an angel man. He guarded the door. All who walked by him were changed by his light. He held a staff. Hearing, "Well, do you want to stay and take care of Stephen or should I continue?" I left.

I learned how to deal daily with post-traumatic stress syndrome. I learned again how to care for myself, how to live apart and at peace without my son in my home. I didn't know if we would ever be together again outside institutional walls. Living in a scarecrow field, I tried to survive and find substance in my barren life. The God I loved had let me down. I didn't know why He had chosen this time to leave me. It had led to the abandonment of my child and the failure of my marriage. How could a good God let this happen?

The winter had been long and lonely. Slowly, I learned to walk with rocks in my shoes. Stephen had been unconditionally loved during his stay in the interim hospital. He was breathing on his own. He had gained weight and his body had become stronger. The decision was made to bring Stephen back home again. Once again services would be secured, nurses hired and trained, supplies and medications ordered and delivered, and hopefully a system would be created that allowed a substantial break for me on a regular basis.

My personal doctor blessed my new effort. The doctors and nurses at the facility transferred their strength and energy to Stephen and me. It was early March, however, when I found out that Stephen may not be allowed to return home due to "diversification of funding." A financial study would determine if it was cheaper for the system to place Stephen in a lower-care facility or return him home. The blow of system limits knocked us down to unknown depths.

Stephen and I sat on the floor under the wooden cross in the chapel. "God help us." The only thing we could do was hope and pray that God would allow us another chance to be together. There were many children who continued to live in this and many other institutions. Many nights I had witnessed mothers and fathers sobbing as they left their children in the care of others. Many times I had walked past the doors of children who were crying or staring blankly at the ceiling or looking about their empty room. Many times I had spoken with parents who tried to reason with the system's shortcomings and make some sense of its destruction.

The caregivers in the institution gave their time, their hearts and their lives for the children that lived in their care. They gave their best to the children. Their best didn't replace the tender love and care that occurs inside of one's home. Somehow I would have to trust in my shattered faith and my mother's beliefs. We would have to wait. If God chose to allow my son to live in another institution, then I would learn to be "mom" in that way. My heart ached to think that he would move again and all-new caregivers would handle him. It would be different

if he could motion for them to come when he needed something. It would be different if he could push them away when
something hurt, or call to someone when he was alone. The cry
of his heart was silent to most everyone.

During that time of unbearable pain, I met two of the finest
people that I know as I sat and drank coffee at a neighborhood
restaurant. It was close to my home, on the road to where my
son was institutionalized. One morning I had gotten an early
start on the forty-mile trek to visit Stephen. Normally when I
stopped in, the restaurant was busy with its breakfast rush.
Now it was quiet and the server, who had waited on me many
times before, saw something in my face that she chose to
address. "Are you okay? You look so sad. Is there anything I can
do to help you?"

The kindness in her eyes and compassion in her voice
soothed my aching heart. Soon Ann sat alongside me with her
daughter, Mary Kay, across from me. They held my hand as I
sobbed and told them of my plight with my son. They told me
of Mother Mary whom they would summon for help and of Her
unparalleled love for mothers and children. They placed a
rosary in my hand with instructions on how to use it, hugging
me and praying with me as I left to visit my son.

New hope had been found that morning through sharing.
They had expressed their love for Jesus and said that Mary
would tell Jesus of my desire to care for Stephen again in my
home. They knew that He would hear Her.

Seven days later the red tape unraveled. Funding was
received, a good nursing service was found, and we were,
thankfully, beginning again our journey home.

The voices were loud and the music entrancing
As they sang and they danced to a crowd that surrounded
The place was well packed with bodies galore
And sweat met with laughter all over the floor
The energy created from movement and voice
Echoed and moved in my soul as it pranced
The concert continued with might and with ease
Until everyone present was struck to their knees
They came with yearnings and desires unfulfilled
And trembled and quaked in the fulfillment of needs
What a novel idea of energy en masse
What a waste that we use it to entertain us
How many children and families would be blessed
If we got on our knees and in mass made a pact
To continue to pray 'til death came no more
To unborn and elderly and those in between
How much could be changed by the lives we could lead
Filled with power to challenge the dark deep inside
If energy is created by entertainment and sports
How much could be changed by prayers said en masse
We hope that our life will be free from the press
Of life's inhumanities, of trouble and woe
And yet when it comes to time spent in prayer
We struggle and mumble and choose not to go
To the heavenly closet where change can occur
To release heaven's blessings on all those below
Instead we prepare all our worldly domains
And we shout and complain as our lives fill with pain
Then we choose once again to be entertained
By people on earth and we idolize them
When standing in heaven and yearning to hear
Waits a God who is ready to fill us all up
With peace, love and joy and with laughter unending
With wisdom and knowledge in all that's fulfilling
His provisions unending, His passion unblemished
He waits and He waits and He waits once again
The road blocks would open, the policies would change
The red tape would be shredded, the provisions be plenty
If only in mass we would pray just one time
Like we yell and we scream at a game or a concert
If only one time we would rise up en masse
The world would be changed and our lives would be blessed

CLN

Visit to the Cross

A year had passed since Stephen was discharged from the institution and lived at home again. The area around his stomach where the tube had been placed to feed him had become infected, creating a deep hole in his abdomen. Pain medication was given but discomfort remained. Every movement caused more pain.

He wanted to go to the cross today.

I had first learned of the cross from co-workers at my new job. We met with one of them for breakfast before going to the cross. Stephen loved the company of my new friends from the restaurant where I now worked. I snickered as I told Stephen about my new waitressing job. It had become a necessity after my divorce and rule changes for home care.

When Stephen first came home with me back in 1989, I had been allowed to work for the nursing service that had contracted to care for him. I complied with all their licensing requirements and followed their structure for my care of Stephen. Six months later, a rule had been passed that disallowed financial compensation through Stephen's home-care agency. The rule involved anyone who was receiving compensation for children in their own homes. Had I continued to work in the hospital or if I worked for the nursing agency and cared for a child in someone else's home, I would have been paid for my services. Now it was being called a "conflict of interest."

Two of my friends, also nurses, had brought children home to live with them. Each one of us complied with and followed all the rules. Millions of dollars were being saved by caring for these children out of the hospital. Millions! Now both my friends faced the possibility that they could no longer continue to care for the disabled children in their homes.

One of my friends continued to care for her child for three more months. She is an attorney now. She left her nursing career with a broken heart and now works as an advocate for abused children. The child she cared for died in her arms that winter fighting pneumonia.

My other friend continued to care for her child for four months in her home. When her savings ran out she had no choice but to return her promise. After returning her child to the hospital, she was in a car accident on her way home. She died. A witness said she was sobbing just before she died, repeating, "I am so sorry, Danny. I am so sorry." Danny lived another three months and died from a rare strain of bacteria common to hospitals.

I wonder how many lives have been affected by rules stemming from the so-called "conflict of interest" clause. I wonder how many children live in hospitals, nursing homes, children's homes, rehabilitation facilities, and foster-care placement that could have stayed home with financial compensation. I wonder how many elderly, dying, diseased, disabled people could have remained home or been returned home with adequate financial assistance. I wonder how many government programs, instead, rob children and adults. Many of the programs were originally designed to assist those with special needs, but their good intentions have been subverted by mankind's greed.

I am happy with every program in place that provides for Stephen's many medical needs. Without them Stephen would not be able to live at home. Somehow, we had been blessed. We were both alive and granted a second chance. Stephen had been able to come home.

I worked part-time in the restaurant with my friends. They had understood that nursing services cannot always "staff the case" even though it is "their job." Nurses in your home come from different backgrounds and some are not familiar with the life-sustaining equipment. Many hours of orientation are required by the family. Children of nurses and nurses themselves become ill and need medical care just as the chronically sick do. Because of this, often at the last minute, I was not able to get to work. These friends had blessed me by giving me the opportunity to work and were understanding of my difficult circumstance. They helped me feel worthy in society again. Talking with other adults about non-Stephen-related things was healthy. My tunnel vision had broadened. This time I did not think that the light at the end of the tunnel was a train.

Arriving at the cemetery that sheltered the old wooden cross, we were greeted by our prayer friends. It was a warm Chicago day. The sun was bright and the weather dry and hot. There were about a hundred people present.

Prayer requests were written down and attached to balloons. Each person held a balloon. Each balloon represented one of the beads in the rosary. We formed a circle around the cross. I brought Stephen to the cross for a closer look. We stayed there, his wheelchair snuggled up close to the foot of the cross that bore a wooden statue of the crucified Jesus. All around us there were people holding balloons. After a word of prayer, the rosary began. Each person prayed a part. The refrain of the rhythmic prayer soothed my hurting spirit. Stephen rested.

Striving and restlessness were silenced.

I stood at the back of Stephen's chair and held his hand close to the wooden cross, using my other to shield him from the sun. One of the older ladies offered Stephen her umbrella for shade. We thankfully accepted. Another young woman came from the circle and held the umbrella over Stephen's face and said, "It's not every day that I can hold an umbrella for an angel."

Under the red umbrella, we accepted the shade. *Drip, drip, drip.* We moved the umbrella to feel the cool rain. The drops were falling on the umbrella and we wanted to feel their cool relief. The sun's glow was blinding! Squinting we moved the umbrella back over Stephen's face. *Drip, drip, drip* continued. The drips were oozing through the umbrella onto Stephen.

Neither the young woman who continued to hold the umbrella nor I could believe what we were seeing. Even more unbelievable, Stephen's stomach had stopped bleeding and he was sleeping—sleeping for the first time in over forty-eight hours. He was breathing without difficulty, his stomach was not bleeding and he was asleep—peacefully resting at the foot of the wooden cross.

In my excitement I ran to get Stephen's nurse who had accompanied us there that day. Seeing Stephen lying so still, she thought he had died. She ran out of the circle, letting go of her balloon. It soared up and hit a branch. A loud pop was heard and the circle's continuity was disturbed.

Soon a small group of people surrounded Stephen, forming an inner circle around the outside circle. The rosary continued. While Stephen's nurse stood over him yet under the umbrella to access him, some of the drops hit her. She began to laugh.

Everyone who touched the drips laughed. We sat at the foot of the wooden cross, in the hot bright sunshine, with drops of liquid falling on us, laughing.

One of the prayer leaders came over to try and quiet our voices. He leaned over Stephen and noticed a tear coming from Stephen's eye. He was still asleep. The leader removed the umbrella and looked up at the cross. The statue of Jesus was tearing, too. From His eyes flowed a liquid that fell onto Stephen and eased his hurting body. To the rest of us it brought laughter.

Another one of the leaders came to the inner circle and tasted the liquid. "Salty," he said. "These are the tears of Jesus."

Grief flows in and out like the tide
Its movement is constant and complete
Its power forces change to all in its path
It strikes without forewarning
It will take you in its grasp
And lead you to the path
Where heaven's soft wind
Meets the earth's warm embrace
It is not kind enough to kill you,
Although you think it may
When you are ready, if you dare
Ride the waves themselves
Peek at the meshing colors of heaven and earth
And learn from the source of life
Forever you will be changed
Riding on the waves of grief

CLN

Identity Crisis

It was a miracle that Stephen was alive.

Three months earlier he had been readmitted to Chicago Children's Hospital. His hips were a constant source of pain. Further tests and x-rays showed his hips rotating out of their sockets, displacing the body's proper alignment. They misaligned to such a degree that his spine and rib cage had shifted very slightly. The body's glorious workmanship had been disrupted. Feet were designed to bear weight, thus preserving the hip joints.

Stephen, like many other children, often required surgical intervention to stabilize infrequently-used joints. The shift of his body's stabilizing bone structure made surgery a necessity. Without it, his bones would continue to shift, dragging internal organs along with them.

Stephen entered the hospital the morning of his surgery. Previously the pre-op testing had been performed at home so he could sleep in his own bed the night before the operation. This time we arrived at the hospital at five o'clock in the morning. Nurses, anesthetists, surgeons, and hospital chaplains greeted us, each one sharing with us their piece in this delicate work. Dressed and prepped, Stephen was ready for surgery.

I wished that my body would be the one to endure another painful procedure. Sharing my hurt, the anesthesiologist began to hum "Jesus Loves Me" as he placed his hand on Stephen's head where mine was. He smiled at me. He began to sing out loud; then the nurse and tech joined in. The sound of their voices faded as the big wooden doors to surgery closed before me.

I paused and looked at these doors in front of me. Many times before I had sought refuge at the foot of a wooden cross. Today in my heart I carried the cross to the surgery doors and left it there. Again I offered my son to Jesus; His will be done. I would thank and praise Him for His work, regardless of the outcome.

The hospital Waiting Room is a refuge for weary pilgrims. Everyone who enters arrives with expectations and anxiety. Time stands still as we wait for our children. We leave them in the hands of qualified people who cut and prod their fragile bodies. Executives cling to stuffed toys, lawyers read Dr. Seuss, pilots play with Tinker Toys. Some choose to sit alone with their memories. Others chat with one another. Some share space with other family members; many sit alone. Some read, work or watch TV. All are in a room that symbolizes vulnerability.

All of us are temporarily exempt from ordinary worldly activities. The rush to get ready for work in the morning is replaced with grabbing a quick cup of hospital-made coffee and a cold face wash. We settle for worn, wrinkled clothing. We hurry to get back to our children's bedsides or rise from our chairs that nestle next to their bed rails. Attentive yet sleep-deprived, we make life-and-death decisions. Trying to look fresh and remain in control, devoid of contact with the outside world, we speak with professionals who now map the future of our precious little ones. Isolated and alone, we smile as procedures that inflict pain progress without complications.

Sitting in the corner of the room was a lady who had not moved from her seat for the last four hours. She sat alone. She hadn't looked at a magazine or watched TV. The only time she spoke was through an interpreter to a nurse. Digging through my bag, I found some candy canes and offered her one. She accepted it as if it was the greatest gift she had ever received. I offered them to others. The small pieces of striped candy chipped away some of the anxiety in the room. Soon the room was full of chatter. During those precious few minutes the inhabitants of that Waiting Room were not alone. The candy cane, a simple piece of candy, soothed our aching hearts and melted our differences. We found strength in our sharing.

One of the nurses in Stephen's surgical team came to the Waiting Room door and motioned for me to come. I gulped as I rose from my chair. I walked with her to the big wooden doors. "There have been a few problems. Stephen is doing okay; he is very stable and he hasn't lost very much blood." I rested on the wall as she continued. "The shelf of his pelvis was cracked. It has been grafted to restore its strength so the hip replacement could be performed. He has needed releases of the supporting tendons and one of them needed a tendon transfer also. Doctor has canceled the rest of his surgeries for the day and we anticipate being in the operating room for another three to four hours." Then she walked back behind the wooden doors.

I stood by the wall attempting to gain support. A man, who had been waiting in the room next to surgery since the early morning, walked toward me. He reached in his pocket and handed me a candy cane. I looked at it, smiled and reached for it. He continued to hold one end of the candy cane as I held the other. We walked back into the Waiting Room together, linked by the candy cane.

Four hours later a flurry of activity passed the Waiting Room doors. It was a bed surrounded by tubes, wires, monitors, IV bags, and people, all totally obscuring the view of the child that lay there. Behind this entourage walked Stephen's surgeon. He removed his surgical head garb and mask as I walked toward him. "Let's sit down for a minute," he said as he led me to a private consulting room nearby.

I wanted to follow Stephen. I had been waiting so long to see him and offer him my support in whatever way I could. Stephen's surgeon offered me his hand. I turned away from Stephen to walk with him and heard, "Jesus loves me . . .." The hum of that familiar tune faded as Stephen's bed turned the corner.

Stephen's surgeon proceeded to tell me about his surgical procedures, pausing to marvel each time at how stable he was. Complication after complication was explained. Each incident ended with, "He remained stable."

We walked together toward the ICU Waiting Room. There I would wait for the many hands involved to settle him in his ICU room. I paused and looked at the wooden doors of the OR. Affixed to the doors I saw a gold cross. Small drops of red fluid were suspended in the air below the horizontal bar of the cross. "With His stripes we are healed." The price of healing had already been paid in full.

I watched the sun set behind the tall city buildings from the ICU Waiting Room windows. Finally the phone rang and one of the nurses invited me in to see Stephen. He lay in the middle of his bed with many wires, tubes and monitors attached to him. He was breathing on his own. I sat down by his side and kissed his cheek. The nurse told me he was still under anesthesia's spell and would not respond. I kissed him anyway. I wanted his little spirit to know that I was by his side, his return of affection was not expected. It never had been.

Night had come to the rest of the world but in the ICU, time knows no day or night. Cares consume minutes. Stephen woke up that evening about 9 p.m. When he awoke he looked at me, smiled, then cried. He was experiencing incredible pain. Stephen had a very high tolerance to painful stimuli. Previously he had astounded the doctors when pancreatitis consumed his body as he presented with a stomachache. Another time he followed prompts from his neurologist, who later found that he was having continuous seizures and suffering from intense intra-cranial pressure.

This night his body felt the overwhelming pain. The nurse soon increased the pain medicine that flowed to his body through a tube in his spinal cord and with it came relief. It brought sweet relief. The next four days Stephen spent in the ICU recovering from the surgery. Then he was moved to the orthopedic floor. I was reminded that each day would bring healing. More healing would mean less pain.

When Stephen cried, the only comfort I found was the picture of the golden cross on the wooden operating-room doors. The suspended red that hung scattered at the foot of the cross became my focus. I continually meditated on its power.

Post-op day six came and Stephen's anesthesia line needed to be removed to avoid infection that could complicate his progress. Pain medication would be provided intravenously. The spinal catheter was removed without difficulty.

An hour later Stephen began to cry. He sobbed and sobbed. His face and hair were wet with tears and sweat. Mine were too. The doctors tried to increase his pain medication, but Stephen's respiratory drive decreased. They even tried to anesthetize his body and breathe for him with an artificial ventilator, but Stephen's airways refused. Instead of accepting the forced air they spasmed, making his already compromised breathing worse. The conclusion was, "We will have to wait and see. There is nothing else we can do." The familiar dance of wait.

Four days of constant tears engulfed every wakeful moment. Stephen continued to smile through the pain. He would reach up and touch my face as his body shuddered with the aftermath of surgical correction. I would help Stephen fight his battle as long as he chose to fight.

When the amount of pain Stephen was experiencing appeared to subside slightly, another problem arose. He began to bleed, slowly but continuously, from the surgical sites. He was given blood products and IV fluids to combat the fluid loss. His body had a difficult time assimilating the fluids, which further complicated his recovery. He appeared to feel better, but his condition worsened and his prognosis was grim. Monitors beeped and a steady stream of normally difficult-to-locate experts filtered into his room.

Over and over, I was told, "His condition is very serious but we have it under control." The words were empty as they said them, while the crash cart containing emergency interventions was wheeled in. I stayed at Stephen's side, singing and reading to him. A steady stream of doctors and nurses flowed in and out of Stephen's room. Seven tense hours passed and the bleeding stopped.

During the time Stephen spent in the hospital we were visited by clergy from our home church. The unexpected help, emanating from prayer, helped keep us strong. Months earlier we had started going to Calvary Church where we felt at home. The church had a genuine passion for salvation and a tenderness toward missionaries. Stephen and I had many missionary friends with whom we kept contact and supported in any way possible. Some of the first stories I heard about missionaries were during my grade-school years. My cousin was a missionary. It was simply a belief I grew up with: "When God gives you the ability to help someone, you do it." Plain and simple, you just do it.

The day following Stephen's acute medical setback we were introduced to a man who would be Stephen's main doctor for the next six weeks. He would coordinate Stephen's care and his six specialists. He introduced himself to me and said, "How long has it been since you went for a walk? How long has it been since you felt the wind as you walked? I need to look over Stephen's chart, and from the size of it that will take me awhile. I will sit right here next to Stephen as I work. You go now. Be back in half an hour and I will tell you our plan." He instructed the nurse to have his calls forwarded to the phone next to Stephen's bed. I leaned over, kissed Stephen and walked out of his room. I was convinced God had sent an angel to care for Stephen and me.

I walked out of the hospital that afternoon through the Emergency Room doors. I welcomed the city smog. The vastness of space greeted my narrow thoughts. As I walked, I felt every tiny breeze, saw every glimmer of light. I saw the world as Stephen did when he first came home from the hospital. Everything was new. I crossed the street to one of the many coffee shops that lined the streets surrounding the hospital. Clever entrepreneurs knew that the long hours spent in the nearby hospital would sell a lot of java.

Crossing the street, I became aware of a man running down the middle of the crowded roadway. "What are you doing?" I screamed. "Get out of the street!" The man was followed by another man who trotted at a distance. I kept walking toward the coffee shop. A bright reflection caught my attention—the man was carrying a gun.

"Not today. Not now. It's my half hour off!" I shook my head and continued to the coffee shop. When I arrived at the counter inside the shop, no one was there. The door was open but no one was visible. I yelled, "Hey, anybody in here? How about some coffee?"

A frightened young girl peeked out from behind the corner. "Don't shoot me," she pleaded. Surprised, I told her all I wanted was a cup of good coffee. I told her I had been drinking hospital coffee for a couple of weeks and was hoping for something better.

The flash of police lights and blare of sirens could be seen outside the coffee shop. I could see that the man with the gun was now sitting handcuffed on the ground next to the police car. When I told her what was going on outside, she sheepishly appeared from behind the counter. She looked at me as if at some wild animal. I chuckled, and said, "Gee, I know I've looked a lot better, but ugly people can have coffee too, can't they?"

She laughed and four other people appeared from behind tables, counters and chairs. Their animated discussion of the robbery that had taken place down the street met my ears but didn't connect. I had been transported to a different time and space with my boy, and danger's face couldn't penetrate it. A policeman entered the shop where I stood at the counter, listening to five people talking all at one time. Their words were interrupted by, "Okay where is she? Where's the girl?"

All five pointed to me. The policeman hustled me outside to his squad car. I said, "Wait, I didn't get my coffee yet!" Later I realized how foolish that must have sounded. Sitting in the police car, I saw the hospital on one side and the coffee shop on the other. What in the world had happened in between these two buildings? Confused, I sat as the policeman radioed his dispatcher that they had "apprehended the accomplice."

Oh, that's what's going on, I thought, and offered congratulations to the officer, who smirked. I still didn't have a clue that he thought the accomplice was me. I thought he wanted my help in identifying the man with the gun. When he began to read me my rights, I was jolted into his reality. "Wait a minute, you've made a mistake. My son is in the hospital and I just came out to get a good cup of coffee."

Another scuffle broke out in the street by the parked police cars and I was moved to the car that housed my supposed partner in crime. "How are you?" I asked. (What else do you ask someone who you just saw running down the street with a gun on a Sunday afternoon?) We waited together in the police car, silenced by an officer. Then I was escorted back to the first squad car. I noticed a large crowd of people pointing and gawking at us. *Eie-yai-yai!* All I wanted was to give my adrenal glands a rest, and here I was about to be arrested.

I told the officer I had to go because my half hour was almost up. Like a scene out of a movie, he said, "The only place you're going, lady, is the police station." I continued to talk with the officers, and eventually they realized that perhaps they had made a mistake. They decided to go into the hospital and see if there was a child named Stephen admitted on the orthopedic floor. As one of them approached the Emergency Room doors, a lady came forward. She spoke briefly to the officer. They pointed to us sitting in the car, then pointed to the hospital. She handed him something and he smiled. Then he shook the lady's hand and returned to the squad where he held out a candy cane. "Sorry. I'll come by and talk with you later. You're free to go."

I walked back to the hospital and up to Stephen's room— without my coffee—holding the candy cane. Dr. R and Stephen were listening to one of Stephen's many Indian flute tapes. He remarked at how soothing the music was. He shared with me the proposed plan of recovery for Stephen. He gave me his office number, beeper number and home phone number. Rare gifts had been given to us that day—Stephen had a skilled coordinating doctor and I had a support wrapped up in doctor's clothes.

Late in the evening a police sergeant came to Stephen's room. He carried a cup of java! "Yea, my coffee!" I exclaimed. I introduced him to Stephen and we sat and chatted as the busy room continued its activities. He was very apologetic. I laughed as he read a part of the report aloud. "Her alibi: 'I just wanted to give my adrenal glands a rest.'" He also was amused when I informed him that his was not the first security group to make a mistake.

~~~

In 1990, Stephen and I had moved into a Victorian mansion in Saint Paul, Minnesota, that we rented from friends who were missionaries in Uganda. After modifying the house to accommodate Stephen's medical equipment, we had moved in. A constant stream of people entered and exited from our home at all hours of the day and night. Teachers, therapists, social workers, delivery people, and caregivers—some stayed for minutes, others for hours.

One night Stephen's nighttime nurse called in sick. I was not a happy camper and was tired. Stephen finally, after much encouragement and many medical cares, went to sleep. I hoped that I, too, could lay my head on his crib and rest. I prepared all of his necessary medications for the night and completed the last equipment maintenance.

I was walking toward the front door when suddenly the quiet was disturbed by a loud bang! Someone broke the door down. I scooted up the steps to protect Stephen but was stopped by, "Hold it right there." In front of the voice that delivered that message was a big gun.

I couldn't believe it; I just wanted to rest while Stephen slept. I turned to this man and told him, "You picked the wrong night, buddy, to get me riled up. I'm tired and I am going to my son's room to take care of him. Take what you want and leave! If you wake him up, *you're* going to put him back to sleep!" I turned and walked up another step.

He persisted: "Listen, lady, I don't want to use this thing, so just hold still."

My dog Shadrack was barking hysterically and it was only a matter of time before this noise would wake Stephen. The others in the group were rummaging about the house. *BEEP, BEEP* blared from Stephen's alarms. I looked at the man who still pointed the gun to me and said, "Thanks a lot, mister, now you've done it. He's awake!"

I followed the alarm to Stephen's room and this man followed me, his associates trailing behind. "Great, just what we need—a 3 a.m. conga line." Stephen was crying. The man who followed me stopped abruptly in Stephen's doorway when he saw the medical equipment and supplies. His abrupt halt caused the others behind him to run into him from behind. It was actually amusing. The lead man screamed, "Stop, everyone. Abort!"

Stephen was startled and cried harder. I scooped him up and tried to comfort him. The man shook his head and said, "Why didn't you tell me?"

"Don't start with me, mister," I replied. He continued to shake his head as he walked out of Stephen's room and gathered his crew. They talked for awhile as I settled Stephen. Sleep was out of the picture for tonight. The midnight matinee was, "We blew this one." I learned that these night intruders were actually police officers investigating an alleged crack house.

"Wise cracks, maybe," I suggested.

The officers helped me carry Stephen down the steps. Another member of the conga line carried his necessary equipment. Once downstairs one of the dancers held Stephen, one petted the anxious dog, while still another put the front door back on its hinges. After the Conga Line Incident, the officers often stopped by to check on us.

~~~

Meanwhile, the Chicago police sergeant, who had brought me coffee, had to leave before I could tell him about another interesting incident with officers of the law. But each day for the rest of Stephen's hospital stay, a policeman would bring me a cup of good coffee.

Stephen continued to heal. The final adjustments were made to his body cast. It was made in two pieces, front and back. That way, if a medical crisis occurred, attending personnel could remove the front of the cast to access his chest. I learned how to change his diaper and the cotton batting that lined the inside of the cast when it became wet. A new wheelchair arrived that allowed him to lie flat. When medications and supplies were delivered and nursing personnel were in place, we packed up and headed home.

Stephen's new cast and painful healing process compromised his respiratory status. His already high level of care elevated even more. We had two choices—deal with his increasing needs at home where we were comfortable, or leave him in the hospital. He had already caught a cold in the hospital, and we chose to stay home before another would attack. He slept all night long when we arrived home—the first full night of sleep his body had had in two long weeks.

The next day the nurse and I worked for two and a half hours changing the cotton batting inside his cast. By the time we reorganized his room and caught up with routine medications and treatments, it was time for the nurse to leave. Her shift was over; mine alone would begin. Stephen and I thoroughly enjoyed our time together without the busyness of hospital surroundings. We played while we performed his needed cares.

Many days and nights were spent helping the other caregivers with Stephen's cast. One morning I was able to arrange for a friend to help the nurse so I could attend a church service. I was new to the congregation, but they surrounded me in prayer. I went home with added strength and renewed energy.

Sunday afternoon Stephen awoke looking a bit blue. His chest sounds were good, but listening to his heart revealed an erratic beat. I turned up the oxygen and called the doctor. If that rhythm remained and Stephen continued to need more oxygen, I was instructed to bring him to the hospital for evaluation. At 4 p.m. I loaded him into the van in his cast and drove to the Emergency Room. At 9 p.m. Stephen was admitted to the Cardiac Unit and placed on telemetry. We completed the admission procedure, which included an extensive in-service about Stephen's cast care and positioning. Signs were hung explaining the importance of keeping his cast on. Many different doctors stopped by to learn and understand Stephen's basic routines. Finally at 5 a.m. I left the hospital for a quick trip home to let the dogs out, grab some clothes and return.

The phone rang as I walked in the door. It was a nurse from the Cardiac Unit. She said the nurse that was attending Stephen had to go on a transport and she had a question to ask me. The grandfather clock chimed 6:15 a.m. I had made good time out of the city. She said, "Stephen is crying and I don't know what's wrong."

I began to go through his possible irritants from head to toe. When I began to talk about positioning, she said, "Don't worry about the cast. I took it off. It got wet inside." I dropped the phone. It hit the floor and we were disconnected. I could not believe what I had heard. I had left Stephen's bedside for seventy minutes after instructing six different people about his cares for eight hours—and now his cast was off. And she wondered why he was crying.

I called the hospital but no one could find Stephen's nurse again. I raced around feeding animals and throwing clothes in a bag. I left the house, sad that I couldn't walk the dogs or play with the cats. I was very hurt that Stephen was crying and could not tell them where it hurt or how to fix it.

I made numerous calls to the hospital trying to reach someone caring for Stephen, but without success. No one seemed to know how he was or where his nurse was. As I sat in rush-hour traffic on the freeway to Chicago, my cell phone went dead.

I stormed into the hospital and ran to Stephen's room. His cast lay on the floor next to his bed; his body shook, his hair was wet with tears. I ran out of his room and grabbed the first gray-coated person I found. A gray coat symbolized the highest rank a doctor could obtain. I dragged him into Stephen's room.

The early-morning ruckus caused quite a disturbance. Stephen's nurse, the one who had called me, ran into the room after us. She said, "What are you doing? Get your hands off the doctor. Are you Stephen's mom?" Nodding Yes, I held onto the gray coat of the doctor. "That figures. He probably wouldn't have so many problems if you were a stable person."

That mysterious invisible line of boundaries had been crossed. I used every ounce of control that my tired emotions could muster. I quickly thought about my options. If I did what I felt like doing, bail money would have to be raised and that would hinder my ability to care for Stephen. If I took him home immediately, we wouldn't find something that could help his heart. *AAAAAAHHHHHHhh.* I looked down at the WWJD bracelet on my wrist—What Would Jesus Do? I let go of the doctor.

The nurse yelled to her superior, "Call Security—we have a crazy one here!" The gray-coated doctor walked to the door, motioned for the head nurse and Stephen's nurse to come close to him. He led them to the foot of Stephen's bed and said, "Cancel Security. Call the orthopedic surgeon." He looked at Stephen's nurse's nametag, pulled out a small notebook and pen, wrote down her name. He looked at the head nurse and said, "Get an orthopedic nurse up here."

She tried to explain hospital policy and correct nursing designations. He looked up from the glasses that sat low on his nose and said, "Now."

He turned to Stephen's nurse and said, "You owe this mother an apology, but don't say a word. You're in enough trouble already. Leave." She attempted to explain how the cast had gotten wet and she hadn't had time to change the wet cotton batting, but the wetness would make his skin break down and infect his stitches . . ..

The doctor interrupted her. "This child has been home for five weeks and each day this mother keeps this cast dry." He pointed to the signs and diagrams that hung at Stephen's head and said, "Leave. Now."

He turned to me and guided me to the chair at Stephen's side. He lowered the side rail of Stephen's bed and introduced himself to him. When the orthopedic surgeon phoned, the call was forwarded to Stephen's room. He explained what had happened and within an hour Stephen was back in the Operating Room. Stephen's hips had, fortunately, not been greatly damaged by the removal of the cast. However, a small portion of the newly grafted area on his pelvis had chipped off, but no further stabilization was needed. He remained in the telemetry unit overnight until the anesthesia wore off. Most of the time he slept. I stayed at his bedside.

We went home the next day with a portable telemetry unit.

He would wear this for seven days. Then a portable device that attached to a phone line would be used to transmit any apparent arrhythmias. Determining the cause and resultant treatment was difficult. The tests showed some possible heart damage. Rest, monitoring and oxygen were already a part of his daily cares.

The next four weeks, Stephen continued to heal from his orthopedic surgery and we sent telemetry transmissions to the Cardiac Unit whenever his heart acted up. Stephen's level of care began to stabilize. Every minute of every day was spent caring, or preparing to care, for him. Short quick social breaks brought much-needed rest. One afternoon as I was caring for Stephen, we listened to one of Stephen's favorite songs, Billy Joel's "Piano Man." We sang and danced—as much as you can dance in a body cast. I marveled at how well he had done.

I had no idea God had more in store. Stephen awoke in his usual fashion. Soon his stretch revealed a small patch of loose skin on his abdomen. I touched it and it just fell off. A two-inch square of skin just sloughed off. When I changed his diaper I noticed some blood in his stool; chest sounds revealed a drastic increase in fluid. His heart rate was irregular and he was having a seizure. I shook my head. One of his systems acting up at one time was enough to handle. Now there were five.

I did my best to relieve his breathing, gave him medication to stop his seizure and bandaged his skin. Still he continued to ooze fluid from his skin, and his need for oxygen increased. Another Sunday afternoon phone call to our doctor. I had found a pediatrician in a nearby suburb that had cared for chronically needy children most of his life as a doctor. He helped with the normal ear infections and immunizations, as well as writing home plans and advocating for nursing hours. His response to Stephen's changed medical condition was similar to mine. I would take Stephen back to the hospital where the experts would help determine his body woes and hopefully assist his recovery.

I packed his things up again. His body seemed to be falling apart around his happy soul. We arrived at Children's Hospital in the early evening. Most of Stephen's regular physicians were not on call. I explained Stephen's procedures, history, and medications to all of the new physicians. At 10 p.m. I asked them if we could return home. They looked at me as if at an alien. I had seen that look many times before. One of the residents asked, "Why do you want to take him home?"

"That's where we live," I replied.

She continued, "No, why do you want to take him with you?" I stood speechless.

Another resident joined her, asking, "Why don't you just leave him here and go home yourself."

One of Stephen's regular doctors entered the room and responded to their conversation. "Obviously you haven't heard about Chris and Stephen. Stephen has been home with her for eight years. They started out in foster care."

One of the residents, astonished, exclaimed, "You chose this?"

I sat with Stephen when they left the room and wondered how they could have missed his beautiful smile. They had been feverishly compiling medical data and they missed this mirror of his soul. The joy experienced at Stephen's side was pure and holy. I was learning things in this life that normally would only be told in the next.

Unfortunately, Stephen had to remain in the hospital. Our pediatrician called and asked if we would stay overnight so his regular doctors could see him the next day. Under protest, I agreed. I hoped to get home so Stephen could sleep in his own bed and be cared for by a nurse that we knew well. I hoped to sleep in my own bed, too.

Not tonight. The nighttime matinee was "admission." Sleep would have to wait—again. At 4 a.m., the admission movie ended. I rested my head on Stephen's bed as he tried to sleep. By 5:30 a.m., Stephen's regular doctors had begun to evaluate Stephen's condition. Each had been called by our pediatrician the night before.

At 3:30 p.m., three of Stephen's specialists came into his room together carrying chairs. Usually it was difficult to get the attention of one them. This was a rare treat. I greeted them and they began: "We have some good news and some bad news."

Before I could choose which I wanted to hear first, they continued. "Stephen needs to stay in the hospital for a course of IV antibiotics. He shows signs of infection; however his white blood count is low. We need to determine the source of infection and then treat it."

I was stunned. I thought they had come to discharge him. They continued, "He will be moved to an isolation room here in the ICU until we determine his infection is not contagious." They walked out of the room. My heart walked out with them.

I leaned over and kissed Stephen and he gave me that familiar smile. His eyes looked into mine with tenderness and compassion. I was reminded that I was Stephen's horse—his ability, his ride on this Earth. This was his journey and I was privileged to travel with him.

We moved to the isolation room where we were met by garbed caregivers. At first their costumes seemed a bit scary. I felt as if we were contaminated. The effect of each interaction was numbed by the barriers the gowns, gloves, masks provided. Smiles could only be seen in their eyes. Stephen's skin continued to slough off, leaving open spaces. I dressed them often to keep them clean and dry. I thanked God that my previous work in the Burn Unit had provided me with the necessary skills to care for Stephen.

Later that day, Stephen's central line was accessed and antibiotics were started. The body cast, the portable telemetry and the IV antibiotics created a bewildering cycle of care. Caregivers worked continuously, providing his body the needed interventions. I helped them as I could and tried to comfort Stephen.

One morning, walking by the nurses' station, I overheard some of them talking about my desire to take him home. They were laughing and saying, "She must be crazy."

Days turned into weeks. My only respite from the busy hospital routines was an occasional outing with one of the hospital chaplains, who had come to Stephen's room one day and said, "Hi, I'm Jenny and you are coming with me for an hour."

I did. Following directions is one of the ways you survive in the hospital scene. We would leave the hospital and eat ice cream, go for walks or get coffee.

Stephen's main doctor came to talk with us late one day. He sat down next to me and said, "Stephen's tracheal culture shows a bacteria that is resistant to all antibiotics. We will try to kill any ancillary infections that are present. Hopefully we will help him feel better. It may buy him some time." He proceeded to inform me about this bacteria. The next few days, I met with infectious disease specialists and signed releases to try new drugs. Intravenous in-services were provided for at-home nursing personnel. Medical ethics representatives spoke to me about "resuscitation limits and decisions surrounding terminal illnesses."

Stephen's body was tiring. He smiled and his eyes were still full of life; his soul did not appear to be affected by the pain in his body. By the time we began the massive preparation to bring Stephen home, my physical strength was wounded. My very being ached. Stephen had been through a lot of medical crises. Each time he had chosen to fight. The fight would result in a compromise of part of his body's systems but he would rally enough to preserve a genuine quality in his life.

This time was different. The first chapter of this book started with limits. The familiar but awkward dance of wait now was replaced with the dance of limitations. It was difficult finding my place in its existence. I didn't know how to dance to this tune yet. I would learn.

The past years had turned me into putty. My desire to care for Stephen at home continued, but my fear of the unknown, compounded by exhaustion and grief, hindered my actions. One of his doctors had to almost throw us out of the hospital. Once we got home, I was okay again. I picked up my heart on the way out of the hospital and advocated for Stephen as I had before. Later that doctor told me that he had "Heard my silent cry." When I was too wounded, he carried my tune.

My little sister Nia called to see how we were doing. She is one of the people who has been by my side since forever. No matter what choices I have made in my life, my mom and my sister have always stood by me. They have given me the free-dom to grow and prosper in their likeness.

Stephen's cares were enormous. We enjoyed being home among our familiar things but I was tiring under the heavy load. The day before Thanksgiving, I set up to give Stephen his eleventh infusion of that twenty-four-hour period. Stephen's positions were limited by the cast. The central-line infusions further hindered his movement. The area around his portacath became swollen and weepy. Often we had to re-access the port, a painful procedure. Numbing medications did not squelch the pain of the needle's insertion. He had a difficult time getting comfortable during the best of times, and his cares interrupted his hard-earned sleep. I couldn't hold him in my arms, as I had so many hours before his surgery and subsequent complica-tions. His cast had been cut lower in his chest area to allow effortless expansion.

The day before, I had called the doctors to ask if we could stop the antibiotic infusions. Frequently Stephen pushed away his caregivers as we administered his IV therapy. Normally he was very easy-going. Stephen's body was weaker, and blood and tracheal cultures showed no improvement. The hospital-borne bacteria that had invaded his body was still present. The best antibiotics in strategic combinations had not eradicated or even slowed the hardy bacteria's growth.

Stephen and I talked about his new disease and found com-fort in familiar things. God is in control and His picture is per-fect, we reminded ourselves. I chewed on the words for hours as a cow chews her cud. I said them easily but their meaning seemed incomprehensible. My emotions were splashed with waves of grief. The possibility of reprieve from disease using these medicines did not occur. Instead his body suffered from the overload of fluid and further respiratory compromise.

Tonight another problem nabbed our attention: his central line wouldn't flush. Attempting to re-access his line brought no relief. At midnight I called the doctor on call. He suggested that Stephen continue the course of IV antibiotics—"That's his only hope." He asked me to call one of the IV nurses to come and place a peripheral IV if she was not able to access his portacath. Stephen's arms, legs, feet, and scalp remained bruised and swollen from the many blood draws and IV attempts. At 1 a.m. I picked up the phone to call the IV nurse. Stephen reached over and touched my arm. I set the phone down and acknowledged the truth that his eyes spoke. No more IVs—not tonight anyway. I bandaged his sore IV sites and stayed with him as he fell peacefully asleep.

When he awoke, I phoned the doctor on call and told him I had not called the IV nurse. I told him Stephen and I were in agreement—there would be no more IVs that night. Many times, being a nurse and mom exposed conflicting values. This was one of those times. I had been trained to follow doctors' orders. I respected, relied upon and expected their orders of care. These orders were reflective of medical ethics and years of developed expertise. This night the differing roles of mom and nurse conflicted. Comfort and continuance conflicted. Suffering shifted. Expecting a medical lecture on the benefits of medicine's best antibiotics, I waited for the doctor's response. It was now 5 a.m.

"Chris, okay," he said. "Happy Thanksgiving. I am on call all weekend, so call when you need to talk. I will contact the hospice nurses and have them call you. They are a good bunch."

Stephen watched me as I got the turkey ready for the oven. Thanksgiving was going to happen whether we were a part of it or not, so there might as well be turkey.

At 10 a.m. the doorbell rang. "Hi, I'm Sue, the hospice nurse. Happy Thanksgiving!" She carried a basket full of food. I stood back to let her enter, amazed at this person coming to our house on Thanksgiving.

She met Stephen, and we chatted for a few hours as she made sweet potatoes, beans, cranberries, and pumpkin pie. Stephen enjoyed her company. It was as if a fresh bunch of flowers suddenly bloomed in our desert. She talked with him about his condition, the antibiotics and his prognosis if he stopped using them. He responded to her appropriately, clearly. He wanted them to stop. He giggled with delight at his ability to communicate with her. Upon command he squeezed his hand for Yes, then he smiled for Yes, then he raised his right hand for Yes and his left for No. I was asked to leave the room and I did.

The same findings resulted. Stephen had had enough of the IV routine. Months previously, he had been asked similar questions about artificial ventilation. Many experts wanted to put him back on the ventilator to ease his diseased airways.

Living with a mechanical machine to breathe is not an easy life. At best, tubes have to stay connected and free of condensation, parts need to stay connected to one another, and a constant power source must be maintained. Many children and adults live with artificial ventilation, and I would like to give each of them a blue ribbon, a Purple Heart, a Grammy and an Emmy award. They deserve great recognition for their accomplishments. The people who assist them should be given the highest award this world can offer, and it still wouldn't be a reward that reflected the level of their compassion and honor. That's why heaven exists.

Stephen had expressed—three different times with three different people in three different ways—that he did not want to be hooked up to his Princess Leah machine anymore. Due to a prominent physician's influence, Stephen was hooked up to a breathing machine despite his personal preference. It did not work. The most sophisticated bifurcation-sensitive ventilator would not benefit Stephen. Instead, it had resulted in a tracheal tear and emergency surgical intervention.

This time Stephen's wishes were respected. Stephen and I had a wonderful Thanksgiving that day, truly thankful for every minute. The next few weeks were filled with medical ethics representatives, hospice clergy and decisions. They told us, "Stephen will not live to the end of the year." The advice we received was, "Get the most out of every day."

We had been enjoying every day for years. We continued as we had.

Heaven's Very Special Child

A meeting was held quite far from earth!
It's time again for another birth.
Said the Angels to the Lord above,
This Special Child will need much love.
His progress may be very slow,
Accomplishment he may not show.
And he'll require extra care
From the folks he meets down there.

He may not run or laugh or play;
His thoughts may seem quite far away.
In many ways he won't adapt,
And he'll be known as handicapped.

So let's be careful where he's sent.
We want his life to be content.
Please, Lord, find the parents who
Will do a special job for You.
They will not realize right away
The leading role they're asked to play.
But with this child sent from above
Comes stronger faith and richer love.
And soon they'll know the privilege given
In caring for their gift from Heaven.
The precious charge, so meek and mild,
Is Heaven's Very Special Child.

Edna Massimilla

Aladdin Genies

This day, Stephen's Aladdin genies were coming. The room was decorated with tiny red and green lights. They hung above Stephen's bed, intermingled with a small school of stuffed tropical fish. As he lay in his bed, he could look up and see the many colorful fish and lights.

The genies entered our house with wrapped packages and good coffee! They talked with us about the organization of the Make-A-Wish Foundation and told Stephen, "We are here to grant you a wish." The beauty of their desire flowed like streams in our desert. They told Stephen they were his Aladdin genies. Whatever he wished for, they would grant. After we opened the presents they had brought and scheduled their next visit, they left singing "Jingle Bells."

The stream continued to wash over us with joy as we entertained the idea of a different kind of wish. A wish to live together outside the hospital had already been granted. A wish to have no more artificial ventilation; a wish to receive no more IV therapy—these had been respected. Now a wish of whatever he wanted? What kind of a wish is that? The idea of the wish itself flooded our hearts with joy. A living wish.

Our new friends Julienne and Ron, the Make-A-Wish genies, stopped by often. It was difficult for Stephen to understand the concept that someone wanted to give him something he didn't need for survival. Most of his life had been spent interacting with people who cared for a part of his body. Seldom did people communicate with Stephen just to play. After many discussions Stephen decided he would like to see the ocean.

Stephen's love for the ocean had begun when I first met him. His restless body was soothed by listening to stories about animals of any kind, but he especially liked learning about the sea and its inhabitants. I had tried to bring the ocean to him by decorating his room with all kinds of fish decorations and toys.

I marveled at the possibility of taking Stephen to the actual ocean. The Make-A-Wish team worked energetically, organizing every detail of Stephen's trip. Out-of-state nursing licenses were obtained, optional airline seating permission granted and housing arranged. An incredible amount of time and effort was needed to move all of Stephen's routine medical equipment, supplies, physician and lab supports to Florida.

That winter, Stephen had been gravely ill. The promise of this granted wish often encouraged him to continue. Finally the day of Stephen's wish had come true. The Make-A-Wish team strived to fulfill every need we had. Every detail had been considered and taken care of. Soon Stephen was flying in an airplane—his first flight ever. He laughed as the plane bounced a little now and then. A cloud flying by brought tears to his eyes, he laughed so hard.

I looked around at the others who we sat with in the first-class seats and saw tears in all their eyes. One man introduced himself to us after the flight, and said as he departed, "I watched your boy laugh and bottled up enough joy to get me through another year. Thanks."

Our trip had only begun but our joy was already overflowing. Everything was picture-perfect. We stayed in a resort called Give Kids the World—the closest place to heaven on this Earth for families of compromised children. For a week we lived in a little city where wheelchairs were the normal means of transportation. Caps took the place of hairstyles and gentle helpfulness met hurting souls. Volunteers sang, read, fed, cleaned, and played with our children.

For one week we lived in a place that felt like a blessing. Upon our arrival we were greeted with cold beverages and warm smiles. Stephen was given a Purple Heart badge. He had survived the winter and made it to his dream destination. He had displayed courage in its purest form. The week would be filled with memorable experiences.

While at Sea World, Stephen encountered a dolphin that he knew. Stephen was positioned onto a dividing wall at the dolphins' swim tank. One of the workers went to get some fish to lure the dolphins' attention to Stephen's area by the wall. When he returned he saw a picture he would never forget.

One of the dolphins had jumped out of the water and lay on the ledge next to Stephen. This dolphin had a big scar on his neck. The worker screamed at us, "What did you do?"

"Nothing," I replied.

"Dolphins just don't jump out of the water for nothing," he said, and ran to the nearest staff station. He came back with an older man who wore a plaid shirt and rolled-up jeans. His silver hair blowing in the breeze, he stopped and stared at us. Stephen had reached out his hand and it rested on top of the dolphin and the two of them were frozen in that position. Judging from the reaction of the first worker, I figured we were in big trouble, so I tried to push the dolphin back into the water. He wouldn't budge. Stephen laughed every time the dolphin wriggled. Quickly apologizing to the man as he approached, I hoped somehow he would understand.

He asked, "How does he know this dolphin? When did he meet him? Was he part of a kid's class or something?"

I explained to the inquisitive man that this was the first dolphin Stephen had ever seen in person. He persisted. "No, when did he see him last?"

I repeated, "This is the first dolphin Stephen has ever seen." The dolphin stayed by Stephen for about an hour. Workers splashed water on the dolphin to keep him wet and cool. When Stephen began to move away the dolphin rolled back into the water. He swam away and returned upright on his tail—chirping and shaking his head directly in front of Stephen's face. It was an unbelievable scene. Stephen watched the dolphin and laughed.

While getting Stephen comfortable again and catching up on his medications and treatments, I marveled at the magnetism the creature had created. Turning away from the water to find some shade, I saw the silver-haired man sitting on a ledge. A young man sat close with his arm around him. I reached out my hand to shake his and thank him for the experience with the dolphin.

He held my hand, looked up at me, and said, "That dolphin was almost dead when we got him. He was stuck in a fishing net and when we tried to cut him out, I accidentally cut him. That's how he got the scar you saw. The net tangled more when he fought to get out and I couldn't free him."

He sobbed as he retold this event. "I waited for him to die. I couldn't free him. He looked at me with those eyes and I couldn't help him. I was running out of air so I had to surface. As I rose through the water, I prayed that somehow, some way the dolphin would be freed. I climbed up the ladder to the boat and was congratulated by Buddy. He said, 'Hey Nick you did it. You got him out.'

"I had no idea what he was talking about. I had left that dolphin bleeding and tangled in a net. Now I saw him jumping and swimming in the water. He wasn't bleeding. He already had a scar! That was last month and since then he hasn't come to anyone. He won't let anyone near him. Your boy talked to him!" The man continued to sob.

As we wheeled away past the man, Stephen dropped his hand over the side rail and touched his new dolphin friend.

When we got home a week later, I looked through Stephen's journal. Stephen had been working on a new auditory scanning device with his teacher. The entry dated 4/19 read, "dolp fre Nic." I raced to the phone and called Sea World. When Nick answered the phone, I said, "April 19—the dolphin—was that the date?" I hadn't even said hello yet.

All I heard was a pause, then his voice: "Yes, that's the date—April 19."

It was time to go to the ocean. The clouds had rolled in, the seas were rough, but we couldn't wait any longer. Packing everyone and everything we needed into the van, we drove to the beach. The sounds of the surf greeted us. Stephen was very excited.

We maneuvered his wheelchair out across the sand to the ocean's edge. We got him out of his chair and onto a raft, the portable suction unit and oxygen tank tucked at his feet. We left the rest of his medical equipment and wheelchair on the shore and pulled Stephen, on the raft, into the ocean. Abundant joy swept over all of us. Every memory of pain dissipated in the steady rolls of the ocean's movement. Every struggle, every disappointment, every hurt disappeared in the soft, salty wind. He was at ease in the water. He was not afraid of its vast expanse. He knew these waters. Somewhere in his spirit and in his soul, he had traveled here before. This was a reunion with a place from a previous journey.

Stephen's wheelchair sat on shore, and for a short time so did all his disabilities. I witnessed heaven. His face glowed and his body's limits dissolved in the sea. I had never thought I would ever see my son enjoy life to its fullest possibility. Now he did—and my wish for him had come true.

A young man stood in a doorway overlooking the beach where we were. He had watched as we placed Stephen on his raft, and after awhile he walked out into the water and stood watching Stephen play. Soon he swam a distance away and, when he returned, stopped by Stephen's raft.

"May I touch his hand?" he asked. Granting him that little wish seemed to release an enormous burden that he had carried. When he let go of Stephen's hand, he held mine and said, "Two years ago my little daughter Emily died right here. She wanted to die where the dolphins played. She insisted on staying here—right here—every single day.

"We would sneak out here in the night and stay all day. Then, about this same time, she got up out of my arms and swam. She didn't know how to swim very well, but that day she swam like that's all she ever did. She giggled just like your young boy. Then, as suddenly as she began to swim, she stopped. She crawled back into my arms as the sun set.

"She waited awhile, looked up at me and said, 'Daddy, I am going to play with the dolphins some more, okay?' I nodded Okay and she died. I haven't left this place for two years.

I wanted to stay right here where she is. Now I know that she swims with the dolphins, like the wind blows in the trees. Wherever there is beauty there is Emily. I can go now. Thank you."

As the North winds blow
May you have wisdom to follow the path provided

As the East winds illuminate your path
May the love of God surround you

As the South winds purify you
May the arms of God protect you

As the West winds blow
May you have peace remembering your travels

> *to Stephen, in honor of the gentle guidance of*
> *travelers in our path*

Red Pathway

Living with the prospect of terminal disease is difficult for all affected: the individual, family and friends, alike. Many times help has come during meditative prayer. A strong, yet peaceful, vision came to me upon one of these occasions, as I struggled to grasp the meaning of Stephen's existence.

The unknown red pathway beckoned my soul. Beneath my feet the soft reddish road cushioned each step. The Earth's steady vibration provided a rhythmic beat and my feet followed its cadence. My body was aware of the flow of life underneath the Earth, yet it remained invisible to my eye. As my feet touched the waves of Earth, my soul was transposed to another time and dimension, each step ordained by another time.

All views of this transposed space were new and comfortable. Lingering in a field of flowers, they lured my attention toward a place on the mountain as the flowers swayed in its direction. They were the inhabitants of this field. The Earth itself nurtured them and they rewarded her with their beauty.

I was a stranger there. A summoned guest. Wolves mingled. Buffaloes roamed freely. Each step was safe, planned before time. Walking up the side of the mountain, I was welcomed by a circular fire. It lit the dark sky as I lingered in its warmth. Time was endless. The smoke from the sacrificed trees rose to the heavens and greeted the generations that inhabited timeless space.

I stood on Earth's vibration in the rising smoke, and heaven's inhabitants accepted the sacrificed gift. My prayers rose.

As the smoke ascended, it greeted heaven and generations of wisdom transcended back to Earth. We were one.

The ceremony continued around me. I was being honored. The beings around me danced and prepared for the journey's transformation.

Soon, I was lured away from the fire by a lone coyote's cry. I climbed higher on the mountain. Around a bend I thanked the coyote for his direction. A blinding light shattered the darkness. It moved upon the face of the Earth, transforming everything in its path. It was sacred. I approached a sharp turn on the reddish path below me. Earth's vibrations pulsed under my feet. Around the bend, the path stopped.

A massive light penetrated the darkness. It was hot, searing, yet did not burn. The light was diffused by a form in the shape of a gate before me. It was a gate of light—thick concentrated light. Its golden color meshed with the source of light behind it. Upon the threshold of this gate, I had to leave my losses. I had to leave Stephen with Another.

This was a ceremony of an event that recognized change as honor. The Light was aware that I left my son in Its presence, forever.

I glanced over my right shoulder and saw Stephen safely nestled in the crook of this mountain. The space was devoid of color around the mountain. Close to the top, a hollowed-out crevice held my son. Beings walked up into the crevice to care for Stephen and were changed by the light as they entered. They were transformed by its power. He was safe.

Nestled in the hands of time, suspended in the space where heaven and Earth meet, the smoke from the sacrificial fire reached heaven's space next to him and ancestors rode on the transcending smoke to assist him. Standing on the threshold of the gate, I was limited only by the steps' depth. Walking with the Earth's movement cooled my feet.

I had been asked—and I had left—the breath of my son to the choice of time.

The gate opened before me. Walking through it, I saw the human world and all its movement. It yearned to feel the Earth's vibration and heaven's peace with possessions and choices of time. It fretted and toiled, creating schedules and clocks that smothered Earth's rhythm. The inhabitants of the world were unhappy.

To my right, I heard the whisper of angels. The gate hadn't opened for a long time and they mused about its promise. The music permeated me and soothed my soul. Heaven was awakened inside me. A single ray of light penetrated my eye, bearing a sense of urgency. Many had been chosen, but few were called. Most do not walk through this gate.

The ceremony continued. The circular fire still burned before me. I took a lock of Stephen's hair, a lock of my hair and sage picked on the mountain path—and braided them together. My hands placed this braid on a clay-stone light altar. As I reached into the altar's space, my hands became as the light gate—matter without physical substance, a light form.

I carried the altar, extended in front of me, over the fire and joined the others dancing. I danced between fire and light and marveled at the constant flow of gentle, purposeful movement. I mingled with Stephen's family, who sat or stood by me.

Out of the firelight, the gate reappeared. Around me stood generations and generations of warriors that mingled in angelic form. The buffaloes' dance was heard in the Earth's vibration as they stampeded before us. With them, they brought the news: "This is the time."

The North breeze brings energy, the East direction. The South wind bears strength and hope; the West wind blows comfort at the journey's final transformation. Seeing Stephen in the crevice of the mountain, I was now aware of the vast, dark-blue space that is time.

The heavens were not a black void but constant movement, transcending limits and creating dimension. From a distance, the same light from the gate behind me, which I had stood in, was now visible in the vast blue space's sky. Multitudes of heavenly hosts entered on the rays of light. My son rested in this space.

As I watched the continuous movement of angelic beings visible in the light from afar, I was met by something ominous— a pure white horse carrying a Man. All the ancestors and angelic beings followed behind this Leader.

His horse stopped in front of me, right front hoof straight and firm and left front hoof bent and raised off the ground. The dust cloud settled underfoot as His ride on the light path paused. The horse's ears stood up, alert to the mission he was performing.

On the horse, the strong Man rode with a white quilt. Many feathers adorned His headdress and a chain of beads encircled His neck. In His right hand He carried a flag. The flag symbolized His powerful authority. He was the inhabitant of time. Behind this mighty Warrior rode many forms of men, women and children. They rode on wings of light and they walked on the winds of the Warrior.

I continued to hold the clay altar that housed my son. The light that created him created me. We were one with every other created being. We had walked side by side in this journey called life, enclosed in these clay altars that are named physical bodies.

We would dance forever in the deep-blue light of the eternal Warrior. We would have form in the breath of the Warrior, God's wind.

You must not think that I am unhappy.
What is happiness and unhappiness?
It depends so little on the circumstances;
it depends really only on that which
happens inside a person.

Dietrich Bonhoeffer

Thirteen Candles

I pulled Stephen up onto my lap and held him gently. This terminal bacteria in his lungs was hindering his other body systems, too. His stomach ached, his skin sloughed and his ears hurt constantly. The antibiotics that he received just took the edge off his discomfort. The smart bacteria, having mutated, had become an entity all its own. The best doctors, the best medicine and the most advanced treatment had held this "bug" at bay, most of the time. Sometimes the bacteria would invade again, and as the flooding water of a bay splashes over the solid earth, saturating its foundation, so, too, this "bug" seeped into the tiny parts of our world.

With Stephen in my arms, we found comfort together. Our souls found strength within. The rest of the world continued in its fast spin as our souls and spirits communed in the quiet place of our hearts. His head lay on my chest and our hearts were comforted by the serene closeness of our bodies. In the full knowledge that each breath was a gift from God, my son rested and slept.

Whenever I left him, his heart rate increased, his chest struggled to obtain air and his temperature quickly rose as his body was challenged to maintain homeostasis. His integral body, with millions of different working parts, was tiring.

Stephen still smiled. He loved life. He had tasted of heaven many different times and today, again, he had chosen life. I wondered why he continued to choose to live in his body when the heaven I had witnessed could mean an end to pain or discomfort.

We were visited by an old doctor friend. We had met Dr. H in December 1992 in Saint Paul, Minnesota. Stephen had been in the hospital fighting depakane-induced pancreatitis. His prognosis looked grim. When his liver began to fail from the acute trauma of the pancreatitis, I asked the doctor for alternatives and was told, "Do anything you want, get ahold of anyone you want. It probably won't make any difference anyway."

Sometimes, the medical profession will think about "alternative" medicine only when they have exhausted their traditional resources. This was one of those times. One doctor put me in contact with another from Mayo Clinic in Rochester, Minnesota. He was working on the effects of nutrition in the depleted body. I spoke with him by phone, explaining Stephen's medical dilemma, and soon he was on his way to Saint Paul to examine him. We had hoped he would subsequently offer help.

I had been writing a letter when the doctor first entered Stephen's room. He stood in the doorway and said, "Chris?"

I heard a familiar voice and turned slowly to look at him. "Dr. H?" I dropped my pen and ran to the doorway where he gave me a warm hug.

"My friend, what are you doing here?" he asked. It had been nine years since our paths first crossed. When I received word from my medical doctors that I had cancer and needed treatment, Dr. H had been a medical student, doing his thesis on "alternative therapies and their effects in early cancer stages." I had volunteered to be a part of his study group and received an experimental treatment under his direction for my early-stage cancer. It had been highly successful for me.

I had had only sporadic written contact with him the previous nine years. Now he was sitting beside me at Stephen's bed, just as he had done years before by my hospital bed. We talked about Stephen and his medical situation. He did offer help.

Stephen's diet became one of plant proteins, carbohydrates, amino acids, and many enzymes. I juiced carrots and broccoli; his tube feeding was laced with garlic. Slowly, Stephen stopped losing weight and his injured liver began, again, its sophisticated detoxification process.

Stephen's resistance to the deadly Xanthomonas virus he had contracted continued to confound scientists. By all measure, he should have been dead—and more than once at this point. But with Stephen's will to live and the careful nutrition that now nourished him, he continued to grow. Bone mass increased, white blood cells replenished—his body seemed to have given the Big X room to coexist within him.

~~~

Dr. H also brought surprising news for me, one Saturday morning. "I have something to show you," he said with a big grin. He retrieved some papers from his briefcase. They were graphs, charts, calculations—pages and pages of incomprehensible data. He pointed to a number on one of his papers and said, "See this? This is you. This is your test page." He talked excitedly, "Look at this. Look at these six numbers. Do you know what they represent?" I shook my head No.

"Six boys with leukemia were saved that year using the same test protocol that you received. Six boys," he said.

My mouth opened and I uttered a big sigh. "What? What did you say?"

"Six boys are alive. You helped," he said. "You let us study your body's reaction to cancer and treatment. Six boys." The thesis he had completed, outlining a new form of treatment for infant and pediatric leukemia, had apparently also been successful. During the first year of the new treatment, six young lives had been spared.

My lifelong dream to be the mother of six boys had come true. My grandfather had told me many years earlier as I bounced on his bed, "Don't ever let go of your dream." I hadn't let go. It just changed shape a little.

~~~

Finally, Stephen was asleep. He was about to be thirteen years old—officially, in thirty minutes. The grandfather clock melodiously chimed that it was 11:30 p.m.

Stephen's nurse and I blew-up balloons and hung them from the tiny lights that wove their way across the ceiling of Stephen's room, over his bed. The stuffed saltwater fish were entwined in the lights, and balloons created a festive display for this special occasion.

Stephen loves the ocean, flowers, trees. He loves being outside and letting the wind blow through his long, black, wavy hair. He catches every glimmer of light before it becomes a rainbow and he hears the bird's song high in the trees. He is happy just being alive.

He looked like an angel as he slept this night. A birthday present lay wrapped by his side, his hand resting on it.

After blowing up dozens of balloons and hanging them with ribbons, I stood in the doorway of his room and marveled at him. He was vibrant and alive—by the grace of God. Stephen weighed eighty-seven pounds and was nearly five feet tall. This young man had begun his life, I remembered, at two pounds and one ounce. Tonight he looked big, strong and peaceful as he slept. At midnight I gently woke him with, "Happy birthday, Stephen. You made it to thirteen!"

Excitement hindered my rest. Stephen's too. He woke up again at four in the morning—laughing. The nurse woke me, as I had requested, and I entered Stephen's room happy to see Stephen rip open the present that still lay by his side. His sweet, silent laughter filled the room. When Stephen laughs his whole body laughs. It's contagious. Some understanding of communication is hindered by his cerebral palsy, but not Stephen's smile and certainly not his laugh! Even his bed moves with his laughter. He opened his present and smiled as his nurse read the title of his new CD, "Billy Joel." His laughter sounded approval and he eye-pointed to the CD player. We had Billy Joel for wake-up.

Years ago Stephen enjoyed Barney and kids' songs. Now, he hand-signed, "Barney's for babies." His preference for music has developed. Barney is out, rap is in. Raffi is still okay sometimes, but Backstreet Boys is okay all the time—at least this week. It has been fun watching Stephen grow up and develop into a teenager—a privilege I never had imagined possible.

When Stephen first came home from the hospital in 1989 he was two years old and his doctors said he would only live for "a few months—maybe." When he recovered from that acute illness, they said, "His body growth will outgrow his lungs' ability before he is four years old." Today he was thirteen!

While Stephen rested and his morning cares were done, I picked-up one of Stephen's favorite friends, Auntie Helene. She and Baby Luke can brighten up any room. She gave

Stephen a big birthday greeting as a kiss quickly got stuck on his cheek. Both of them laughed, that wonderful, filling, healing laugh. Baby Luke sat on Stephen's pillow and touched his face. Stephen giggled as Luke played with the fine hair that now covered his upper lip.

It was noon and Stephen wanted to go swimming. Two years ago Stephen's heart began to fail, an unfortunate result of chronic lung disease. A few months after receiving that news, we moved into a building with a swimming pool available twenty-four hours a day, seven days a week. Our new apartment was a huge blessing; the pool was like chocolate icing on the cake.

We packed everything we would need for swimming and began our short walk to the pool. We formed a caravan— Stephen in his wheelchair and Baby Luke in his stroller. The nurse carried Stephen's raft and my shoulders transported filled bags, medical supplies, oxygen, and towels. A trail of balloons followed us.

Arriving at the pool, the bright sunshine and warm breeze welcomed us. Stephen was excited; he loved to swim. We positioned him inside his raft and pulled him into the pool. His whole body wriggled with delight, free in the water. His feet hung over the side of the raft and he kicked to splash us, laughing as we screamed, "Ahh Stephen, you got me."

Hours passed as friends from the apartment building came by and wished Stephen a happy birthday. Some brought balloons, others offered high-fives and some came to swim with him. Kids hung on the side of his raft and gave him rides. All who came to greet Stephen left with a heart full of joy, each aware they were experiencing a miracle. Stephen's life is the gift.

Back in our apartment, Stephen continued to be greeted by neighbors. All had come with well wishes. A constant flow of people traffic filled the day—including many phone calls from family and friends. The mail brought Stephen another present, which he opened quickly. His Auntie Bonnie had sent him an Hawaiian surfer's shirt. He laughed when he saw it and wanted to wear it—now. I smiled as he signed, "Now, now, now!" Wearing his new shirt, he looked very grown-up. His long hair fell over his shoulder. He sat in his chair straight and tall.

Another present was opened: computer software. Stephen came to full attention when I said the word *computer*. Most of the time when Stephen and I walked through a toy store, we left empty-handed. Either the toys were too young for him or he was unable to operate them due to his cerebral palsy. Switch-toys had been fun at age six, but not now. He had thirteen-year-old interests and the computer was one of them.

We loaded the software into the computer. Stephen hit the switch to activate the mouse as the machine said, "You've got mail!" Stephen loved mail and he moved with delight to hear his mail read aloud. The computer talking to him was great entertainment. At suppertime, as more friends gathered, I had to bribe Stephen with a little chocolate frosting to get him off the computer.

Finally, it was birthday cake time. Uncle Billy held Stephen's cake as thirteen candles were lit. Each candle glowed, signifying a year of miracles and survival. The kids surrounded Stephen's chair and helped him blow out his candles. As the light from the candles dimmed, there was a moment of silence.

The lights came on to many tear-filled eyes as applause swept over us. Spontaneously, we all hugged one another.

It was 9 p.m. and Stephen was getting tired. His day had begun at four in the morning. Back in his bed, he rested, still smiling. I sat by his side and reminded him that in two days we would go to see grandma in Wisconsin. We would go fishing and have a campfire and cousin Brianna would be there to have fun with him. He laughed when I mentioned her name and then gently sighed, knowing he needed to rest. Like any other teenager, he would have liked to stay up with his friends.

Slowly—surrounded by balloons, cards and presents—Stephen drifted off to sleep, as we gave God thanks for a wonderful day and for thirteen beautiful years.

Our ride on the wind continues.